TALK YOUR WAY TO THE TOP

COMMUNICATION SECRETS OF THE CEOs

STEPHEN R. MALONEY

PRENTICE HALL
Englewood Cliffs, New Jersey 07632

Prentice-Hall International (UK) Limited, *London*
Prentice-Hall of Australia Pty. Limited, *Sydney*
Prentice-Hall Canada, Inc., *Toronto*
Prentice-Hall Hispanoamericana, S.A., *Mexico*
Prentice-Hall of India Private Limited, *New Delhi*
Prentice-Hall of Japan, Inc., *Tokyo*
Simon & Schuster Asia Pte. Ltd., *Singapore*
Editora Prentice-Hall do Brasil, Ltda., *Rio de Janeiro*

© 1992 by
Stephen R. Maloney

10 9 8 7 6 5 4 3 2 1

Library of Congress Cataloging-in-Publication Data

Maloney, Stephen R.
   Talk your way to the top: communication secrets of the CEOs /
by Stephen R. Maloney.
     p.   cm.
   Includes index.
   ISBN 0-13-882788-5
   1. Business presentations—United States. 2. Public speaking.
I. Title.
HF5718.M32 1992   92-8888
658.4′52—dc20   CIP

0-13-882788-5

PRENTICE HALL
Professional Publishing
Englewood Cliffs, NJ 07632

Simon & Schuster. A Paramount Communications Company

Printed in the United States of America

DEDICATION

As this book neared completion, my wife Patricia suffered a severe stroke. I have dedicated this book to Pat, who will always be the center of my world. Pat's dedication, love of life, and courage inspire everyone who knows her.

TABLE OF CONTENTS

INTRODUCTION: PRESENTATIONS—WE ARE WHAT WE SAY AND HOW WE SAY IT

"Mary Richards" [Mary Tyler Moore, after having been asked to direct her first news show]: "But Mr. Grant, I have trouble *asserting* myself."

"Lou Grant" [Edward Asner, reading a programming schedule]: "Uhh . . ."

Richards: "*People just won't listen to me.*"

Grant [Looking up]: "Whaddya say?"

As a punster might put it, "If you can't *express* yourself, you'll spend your life riding the local." In other words, if you can't get your points across, the road to success will be long, bumpy, and uncertain. That's the lesson implicit in the dialogue between "Mary" and "Lou."

SMOOTHING OUT THE BUMPS ON THE ROAD
TO SUCCESS

Speaking well in public—to an audience of one, or one hundred, or one thousand—is crucial in making it to "the top."* Why? Because success in life rests mainly on our ability to convince others to do what we want them to: buy our products; support our ideas; see us as credible and informed; and accept us as the right person for a job or an assignment. Words are bridges that link leaders to their followers.

SPEAKING WELL: "IT'S JUST NOT
THAT COMPLICATED"

Much of the advice we get on making presentations focuses on *how* to speak, on delivery—rather than on *what* to say, on content. One book on public speaking presents a list of more than 300 points (!) for speakers to consider before making a presentation. It reminds me of Einstein's comment when asked why he had stopped reading Freud: "Life's just not that complicated." Neither is making presentations.

Talk Your Way To The Top is different. In simplest terms, this book states that we learn to talk well the way we learn to walk well: by trial and error, by knowing where we want to go, by falling down, by picking ourselves up, and by toddling off again. Speaking well in public is basically a

---

*   In this book, I use the phrases "speaking in public" or "making presentations" rather than "public speaking." The phrase "public speaking" has acquired a connotation of ominousness and unpleasantness, something like the phrases "barium enema" or "towaway zone." A presentation is any significant statement made to an audience of one or more.

simple undertaking, one not to be confused with nuclear physics or neurosurgery.

SIX WORDS THAT BEGIN WITH THE LETTER "P"

Making good presentations is a skill, one that just about anyone can learn. It just takes a lot of things that all happen to begin with the letter "p": persistence, patience, planning, preparation, polishing (of language), and practice—lots of practice.

The success of a presentation is the sum total of the efforts that have gone into its preparation.

PRINCIPLES BASED ON EXPERIENCE

The principles in this book derive from the practice of some of the most successful people in the United States: senior executives at major corporations and associations. In my work with such individuals, I've seen how they use effective presentations to gain and retain their positions and to maintain their authority. They have literally "talked their way to the top."

Oral communication is the foundation of business leadership. A chief executive's day is spent doing two things: listening and talking. As Hewlett-Packard CEO John Young puts it, "Most of what a CEO does, one way or another, is communicating with various constituencies."

A CASE STUDY: A MAN WHO WAS AT A LOSS FOR WORDS

It's doubtful that a poor communicator could be a good CEO. Consider a discussion I had with Robert J. Buckley, Sr., the colorful and outspoken former Chairman of Allegheny International. We were discussing an executive who had an outstanding educational record and a thorough knowledge of the company's businesses. He'd been mentioned as a possible successor to Buckley.

"The Board [of Directors] just won't buy him for the job," said Buckley.

I was surprised, knowing that Buckley liked the man and respected his talents. I asked, "Why?"

"He lacks presentation skills," said Buckley. "He'd stumble through speeches in front of the Board or the news media. They'd smell blood and tear him apart."

Not long after Buckley and I spoke, the man in question had left the company. Over the years, I've seen many talented communicators make it to the ranks of top executives, while poor communicators joined the list of also rans. They don't reach the pinnacle because they can't define their positions or strategies; they can't motivate others to follow their lead; and ultimately, they can't convince their superiors to give them top jobs.

THINK ACTIONS SPEAK LOUDER THAN WORDS? THINK AGAIN!

"But," you might ask, "isn't what we *do* in life more important than how we *describe* it?" Think about this in terms of the business CEOs. We've said that their job consists largely of listening and talking. Yes, they also make decisions. But they make them in words, and they communicate them to their followers (subordinates) in words, just as they justify their actions to the Board in words.

In an important sense, actions don't speak at all. That's why, practically speaking, leadership is more a matter of words than of actions.

A KIND WORD FOR HERETICS NEVER HURT

What I've said is a heresy. But think about it: Leaders rarely act; in fact, they have *followers* to act for them.

Leaders define problems and offer solutions; they outline strategies; they motivate subordinates; they critique performance. They do all these things with words.

A lot of people would see General Norman Schwarzkopf as a true "man of action." But is he? During the Persian Gulf War, General Norman Schwarzkopf didn't kill or wound a single enemy soldier. During the Persian Gulf War, he consulted with his superiors and subordinates, helped develop strategy, and gave a lot of orders. He also held two notable press conferences. Then he retired to give speeches (at $50,000 an appearance) and to write his memoirs. A man more of *words* than of *actions*.

IF YOU KNOW HOW "MARY RICHARDS" FELT, THIS BOOK IS FOR YOU

If communication deficiencies are holding you back in your career, this book can help turn your life around. By learning and using a few simple principles, you can improve your ability to speak in public. These are principles put into use every day by America's most-listened to figures.

In the past 20 years, I've worked with approximately 100 senior executives at 20 major companies and associations. At times, as a speech consultant, I've "put words" into the mouths of these powerful men and women. More often, these high achievers have put ideas into my head about the secrets of successful oral communication.

THE CENTRAL SECRET . . .

The central secret I've learned is this: For better or worse, we are what we say . . . and how we say it. We are *homo verbus*, creatures of words, of sounds given form and meaning. The words we use and how we use them define who we are in terms of personal presence, social status, and career success.

. . . AND TWO RELATED SECRETS

The successful executives I've worked with have taught me two related secrets:

- first, great speakers are made, not born; the ability to communicate effectively is *learned.*
- second, as we improve our ability to communicate, we gain in confidence and self-respect.

THERE'S NO ESCAPING COMMUNICATIONS

Few of us will ever have to address a joint session of Congress, but all of us have to communicate at times in social situations: to make reports or comments at business or civic meetings; to deliver toasts at weddings or retirements, to give eulogies at funerals, or to make statements at town meetings.

The principles in this book are for men and women who have to sell products, proposals, or ideas. They're for people who want to find out how to emulate the decisiveness and the persuasiveness of those who occupy the seats of power.

RELEARNING A FAMILIAR LANGUAGE

This book will "demystify" the process of making effective presentations. Speaking in public is not like learning a foreign language. It's a matter of learning to use more effectively a language you've known all your life. It's a matter of unlocking potential you never knew you had.

AN INVITATION TO A JOURNEY

As you put the ideas in this book into practice, you'll find yourself becoming a better speaker. You'll learn the communication secrets that have helped top executives succeed. These secrets are *practical prescriptions* you can use right away to begin improving your presentations. Speaking better might just be the beginning of an exciting journey of self-understanding, personal growth, and career fulfillment.

Points to Remember:

- Success in life depends largely on how effectively we convince other people to take actions we recommend
- The six "Ps" are crucial in effective presentations: planning; practice; persuasive arguments in support of your call to action; preparation; and polishing of your language;
- Great speakers are made, not born, and by reading this book and applying its principles you can start becoming one.

1

PROVOCATIVE MESSAGES: THE ESSENCE OF GREAT PRESENTATIONS

THE FIRST RULE OF PRESENTATIONS?
HAVE SOMETHING TO SAY

A few years ago, there was a movie called *The Krays*. It dealt with two strange brothers who evolved from being nasty little boys into homicidal adults. Early in this generally ghastly movie, however, there's a funny scene. The brothers are drafted into the British army, and we see them and their comrades standing at attention as they endure a tirade by a bulldog-faced British sergeant.

Disgusted by the officer's bluster, both brothers start to leave their barracks. The sergeant asks them what they're doing. One Kray says, "You don't have *anything* to say . . . and you're saying it *too loudly*." Both brothers then knock the sergeant to the floor.

BEWARE OF SPEECH COACHES
BEARING MYTHS

Some writers and coaches have spread a pernicious myth about presentations. They argue that most audiences

1

soon forget what they've heard. Therefore they reason, *what* you say isn't as important as *how* you say it.

For example, consider the position of a well-known firm that offers "speech training" to business executives—at a price of several thousand dollars per day. They tell their clients: "An audience will remember only *1 percent* of what you say. But they'll remember *100 percent* of how you say it."

My experience has been that books and coaches that emphasize form over content usually talk a lot about "maintaining eye contact" with the audience; sometimes they talk about little else. Yes, good speakers refrain from staring obsessively at their text, or at the lectern, or at the ceiling.

GOOD PRESENTATIONS DO NOT LIVE
BY EYE CONTACT ALONE

A speaker with little to say and with even less conviction about the subject, however, will be more likely to look for the exit sign than for the whites of his or her audience's eyes. Good presentations do not live by eye contact alone. My advice would be: Talk directly to the audience. But when you do look at your speech text or notes, make sure there's something there to look at.

LOOKS AREN'T EVERYTHING

The point is: Platitudes and poppycock are not the substance of great presentations. To assert otherwise is a little like saying, "The meal wasn't very good, but it certainly *looked* great."

Think about it: We don't know much about how Abraham Lincoln delivered the Gettysburg Address, but we have long noted *what* he said there. But what if, say, Mrs. Lincoln's laundry list had somehow made its way into Lincoln's notes. Then we might have had, "Fourscore and seven years ago, our forefathers brought forth three pairs of woolen underwear, two string ties, four dress shirts, and one stovepipe hat."

In presentations, content is important. We shouldn't try to divorce content from form, to separate *what* is said from the *way* it's said. In fact, the content of a speech drives the method of delivery, whether it's Churchill's celebration of the Royal Air Force's "finest hour" or Richard Nixon's "Checkers" speech.

Speakers who feel strongly about their subjects are on the way to making a good presentation. The more passion speakers feel about their topic, the more work they'll devote to its preparation—and the more intensity they'll put into its presentation. Conversely, diffidence is a prescription for dullness.

TAKE BORING TOPICS AND MAKE THEM SING!

When most presenters are confronted with the need to make presentations interesting, they say, "Yes, but the topics I get are boring. They don't lend themselves to interesting presentations."

My advice is, don't take boring topics at face value. The person who made the assignment will be in the audience. He or she doesn't want to hear a dull presentation. Neither do the other members of the audience.

A boring topic is a challenge to the presenter, a challenge to make its treatment interesting and relevant. If you're asked to appear at a meeting, for example, to give "a rundown of this quarter's sales figures," you have a choice. You can go through a lot of numbers, detail percentage increases and decreases, come to a conclusion when you run out of numbers, and then sit down to less than thunderous applause.

Alternatively, you can look at the assignment as an opportunity to make recommendations for actions that will be meaningful to the audience. For example, this quarter's numbers differ from the same quarter in the previous year.

Why? What businesses are doing well and perhaps offer the opportunity to do even better in subsequent quarters? What businesses are trending downward and what, if anything, can be done to turn them around?

REMEMBER, YOU'RE NOT TALKING TO YOURSELF

Most important, think about your topic in terms of the audience. Consider how they can influence the course of events you're describing. That is, how can they affect the course of sales figures? Can they provide marketing support? Can they authorize opening new markets? Can they give the sales force more incentives? In short, what can your listeners do about the matters you're discussing?

Don't fall into the trap of just "giving information." In fact, if all you have to give is information, consider not giving a presentation. Hand out the "information" on a printed sheet and ask for questions about it. The opposite course—reading numbers to people—insults their intelligence.

It also reinforces what threatens to become a national malaise: the ordinary citizen's feeling of powerlessness. Most of us get great quantities of "information" about subjects we feel powerless to influence: homelessness, drug addiction, crime in the streets. We don't need information per se. We need advice and insights on how to use information so as to influence events.

When you're given a topic to discuss, you're also being asked an implicit question: What do you have to say about this subject that's interesting and provocative? You're being asked to do more than say, "Here's how it is." You're being asked to say, "Here's how it is . . . and here's what you can do to change it in a positive way."

If you stray somewhat from the topic given, will the person who made the assignment hold it against you? Frankly, I've never heard anyone criticized for giving a good presentation.

THE BEST ARE FULL
OF PASSIONATE INTENSITY

America's best corporate speakers, past and present, are individuals who feel passionately about their subjects. Their numbers include GE's Jack Welch, Chrysler's Lee Iacocca, Aetna's Ron Compton, and Allegheny International's Robert J. Buckley, among others. They are all individuals who have something to say, and that is the key reason why they say it so well.

GE'S JACK WELCH AS EXHIBIT A

For example, Jack Welch doesn't want audiences to remember his "style" or his "presentation techniques." *He wants to use that style and those techniques to get his message across.* The essence of his leadership lies in getting the audience to share his dislike of bureaucracy and his relish for competing in the global marketplace.

UNWRITTEN RULES: MADE TO BE BROKEN

Against the example of speakers like Welch, there's an unwritten rule (one often enforced by company lawyers) in business communications: Presentations should not offend anyone. The theory behind this approach is that if you don't say anything, it won't get you (or your employer or association) in trouble.

So, the theory goes, speakers should tell audiences exactly what they want to hear. In other words, if you're speaking to dairy farmers, tell them cows are not bovine buffoons but rather the apex of the animal world; price "supports" are the linchpin of the rural economy; farmers are the backbone of our society. Don't challenge them; don't raise any controversial issues; and, above all, don't make any references to cholesterol!

If you're tempted to follow this approach, remember that **it's impossible to deliver a thoroughly predictable**

message—an obsequious message—with any degree of
conviction or credibility.

NO WONDER THEY HAVE TO PAY THEM
SO MUCH MONEY

By the nature of their jobs, CEOs have to make a
number of bland presentations. They have to welcome visit-
ing dignitaries and so forth. Bright, imaginative CEOs hate
this part of their job. They don't like to open their mouths
unless they have something fresh and interesting to say.

This point was brought home to me once, when, at the
behest of our "governmental relations" people at Gulf, I wrote
a "Be Sure and Vote" video presentation for Chairman Jerry
McAfee to read to Gulf employees. The text was a "classic" of
its kind, crammed with clichés about citizenship and democratic responsibilities. Gulf's lawyers had blue-pencilled
the remarks to make sure they were nonpartisan and non-
controversial. In fact, the statement was robotic in tone and
content.

When I sent this atrocity to McAfee, he read it and
deposited my speech draft in the trash. He then wrote his
own presentation. It was hard-hitting and heartfelt.

Two of Gulf's lawyers tried to talk McAfee (who held a
doctorate from MIT) out of using his presentation. McAfee,
who gave new meaning to the phrase "doesn't suffer fools
gladly," told them to cease and desist. At that point, McAfee
became one of my heroes.

WHEN TO GRIN, BEAR IT, AND SAY IT

Of course there are occasions when speakers should
not attempt to ruffle feathers. A wedding reception, for
instance, is not the time for the bride's father to tell the
groom what he *really* thinks of his new son-in-law. But even

on festive occasions, speakers should try to avoid clichés and recitations of the obvious.

SOCRATES: "KNOW THYSELF."
MALONEY: "KNOW THY AUDIENCE"

It's important to be clear on this point: *Talk Your Way To the Top* emphasizes the importance of knowing your audience—and of shaping your message accordingly. But unless all the evidence is to the contrary, don't underestimate your audience's intelligence. If you overpraise them, they may determine that the speaker "doth protest too much." If you pander to them, they will eventually resent it.

HOW ARE GOOD PRESENTATIONS
LIKE CHINESE FOOD?

The best oral remarks tell the audiences something they didn't know—or that they didn't know they wanted to hear. They're like Chinese food: Spicy enough to be interesting, but with portions small enough to leave us wanting more. Such presentations evoke a *response*—not a *yawn.*

THREE CASE STUDIES
OF PRESENTATIONAL "WAKE-UP" CALLS

Robert Buckley was asked to speak at a Pittsburgh conference on international trade. Among the foreign visitors were several Japanese industrialists.

Most of the speakers avoided the tough issues of international competition and access to markets. But not Buckley. He noted that some Japanese observers had defended that country's closed markets on the ground that "Japanese culture" discouraged the purchase of imported goods. "In those cases," said Buckley, "the Japanese are going to have to change their culture."

His remarks precipitated some vigorous discussion at an otherwise rather sleepy conference.

AND THE TRUTH SHALL MAKE YOU FREE

In another hard-hitting talk, the new head of personnel at a major corporation addressed some of her subordinates. Her remarks dealt with policy changes she was making. She observed that the personnel function at the company had historically involved developing and processing reams of forms.

"In other words," she said, "we have been a secondary, administrative function."

She added that henceforth the personnel function would emphasize counseling managers about personnel matters directly related to the business needs of the company. "That," she said, "will make our jobs harder and more complex. It will also give our function more stature . . . and give us more status."

Her presentation was a classic wake-up call. To an audience used to hearing predictable praise and "human resources" jargon, she gave a message of real substance. One could almost see the audience's eyes open and ears perk up. It was a stellar performance by an individual not afraid to speak the truth.

A MAN WHO'D HAD "A BELLYFULL"

Bill Douce, former CEO of Phillips Petroleum, was known for his candor. He specialized in saying things his brethren in the industry sometimes didn't want to hear.

During a period of energy turmoil, he told a meeting of the American Petroleum Institute that it was time "to stop bellyaching about the government" as the cause of the industry's problems. He pointed to the industry as the source of many of its difficulties. As the saying goes, "the audience applauded with one hand," but Douce had made his point.

On another occasion, Douce noted that the federal government blamed the industry for the nation's energy problems. On the other hand, he observed, the industry blamed the government. Douce took another approach. He praised the government for its "new realism." He emphasized that government's role was essential "in focusing national attention on problems and on presenting fundamental policy choices."

Douce refused to use the government as a scapegoat. He noted that in many cases business had been "inconsistent" and short-sighted in its advocacy of federal policies. In taking this approach, he helped to heal the ruptured relations then prevailing between the oil industry and the federal government.

CANDOR CATCHES THE AUDIENCE'S ATTENTION

I attended the presentations I've mentioned. What I remember is how well they were presented and how enthusiastically they were received. The audiences at each of them were rapt. Perhaps they were surprised at what they heard: authentic human voices talking with candor and conviction about real issues.

Points to Remember:

- Believe in what you say; otherwise, feign laryngitis.
- Convince the audience to act on the points you make.
- Know your audience, and shape your message accordingly.
- Tell your audience something they didn't know they wanted to hear.

2

THE CEOs, YOU, AND SELF-IMPROVEMENT

Are the CEOs who become strong communicators really that different from you and me? Recall the (reported) conversation between writers Scott Fitzgerald and Ernest Hemingway. Fitzgerald, dazzled by the lives of the affluent and famous, observed solemnly to his fellow author, "The rich are different from you and me."

The less easily impressed Hemingway said, "Yes . . . they have more *money.*"

If those who seize the brass rings of American business are different from us, it's perhaps because they have a more expansive view of the "limits of the possible." The CEOs are passionate believers in their potential for self-development.

Like James Thurber's Walter Mitty, they can visualize themselves performing great acts. But unlike Walter Mitty, they take the steps necessary to make their visions real.

WHY CEOS HAVE TO BECOME
GOOD COMMUNICATORS

Advancement in any organization depends largely on communication skills. At the lower levels of large institutions, communication skills are less important. That's because the individual starts as a worker with assigned tasks: a mail clerk, an insurance underwriter, an engineer, or an accountant. The tasks are well-defined and involve producing some measurable output.

As individuals become managers, they stop producing these "products." Instead, they manage people who generate products. And what is management? It involves selecting and evaluating personnel; it involves "coaching" and motivating people; it involves communicating the organization's policies and strategies.

Essentially, management involves transmitting information. It entails some writing and a lot of talking—to subordinates and superiors. The higher up managers go, the more their jobs become a matter of listening and talking. At the top levels, managers find themselves making a significant number of presentations, external and internal. They may be making these presentations to trade associations, customers, financial analysts, and government regulators and legislators.

Some of the senior executives discussed in this book have 50,000 or more people "reporting" to them. There's no possibility they can talk one-on-one with all their subordinates. It's unlikely they can even get to know more than a fraction of them. So the CEOs have to delegate responsibility, which involves making (and listening to) presentations. CEOs also find it necessary to make presentations to their entire employee constituency.

As they make their way up the ladder, most executives struggle to communicate effectively. Many of them have majored in accounting, finance, engineering, and business—subjects not noted for producing good communicators. These individuals have to do whatever is necessary to become good communicators.

HOW MUCH TIME TO BETTER COMMUNICATIONS? LESS THAN YOU THINK

Is it as difficult as you might think to become a person who makes good public presentations? Most people could be better communicators—if they made the effort. How long would it take them? If they follow the principles in this book, they could make dramatic improvements in a day or two. If they worked on it for a week, the improvements would be astounding, visible to all those around them.

Why are there so many bad presentations and so few good ones? More to the point: Why do people who've given many presentations continue, year after year, to blunder through incoherent remarks?

I believe the answer is simple: Most presenters don't learn the basic principles that underlie good presentations. Instead, they learn bad habits. Then, they reinforce these dubious practices every time they speak in public.

GOLF TEACHES A LESSON
ABOUT COMMUNICATIONS

Such individuals remind me of the people we see on golf-driving ranges. I refer specifically to the 250-pound individuals with massive forearms. They look as if they could pulverize a golf ball.

However, what actually happens? More often than not, they grip the club too hard, their veins nearly popping out. They stand stiff-legged, magnifying the tension in their bodies. They bring the club back too fast; then they take a swing so prodigious that their legs, shoulders, and head jerk up, and their left foot comes off the ground.

Once in a while these people make the ball fly out on the range, usually slicing to the right. Most often, they hit the ball on the top and it trickles a few yards off to the left.

Contrast this performance with what we see when we visit the Ladies Professional Association tournament every year. We see many women who are little more than 5 feet tall and 100 pounds. They grip the club firmly but without tension; they make a nice turn of their shoulders and hips on the backswing to generate power; they keep their heads steady; they swing the club with ease and seeming effort-lessness. And the ball usually flies 220 yards or more.

Why can these "little women" in sun visors out-hit the beefy behemoths of the driving range? Because they have learned the basic skills by taking golf lessons—something that would never occur to the driving-range duffers. Because they practice trying to hit the ball solidly rather than trying to knock its cover off. Because they realize that any easy, rhythmic swing will produce better results than the ferocious cuts taken by the beer-belly set.

GOLF: KEEP YOUR HEAD DOWN; COMMUNICATIONS: KEEP YOUR CHIN UP

In making presentations, most of us bear more resemblance to the driving-range duffers than to the women professionals. And in communications, as in golf and tennis, the remedy is the same: Take a few lessons (that is, read this book), learn good habits, and reinforce them through practice. Take my word for it: It's a lot easier to give good presentations than it is to win the U.S. Open!

Learning to speak well, like learning to hit a golf or tennis ball, takes commitment; it takes work; it takes practice; it takes a willingness to recognize our strengths and weaknesses and to turn the latter into the former.

JFK: IF THY LEFT HAND OFFEND THEE . . .

Take the example of John F. Kennedy, one of our finest political orators. Most people would be surprised to learn that Kennedy, especially in his early years, was very nervous about speaking in public. In fact, when he did so, his left hand shook so much it was noticeable.

How did he deal with this problem? He put the shaky left hand in his pocket, while he used his unshaking right hand to gesture with "vigah." By accepting hundreds of speaking engagements, Kennedy confronted his particular "devil," his fear of public presentations. Ironically, Kennedy's putting the unruly left hand in his pocket was interpreted by viewers as one more sign of the famous Kennedy casualness.

"THERE ARE NO PROBLEMS, ONLY OPPORTUNITIES"

I've heard more than one CEO intone these words: "There are no problems, only opportunities." This belief reflects their ability to look at adversity as a challenge, a trait exemplified by many of the executives with whom I've worked. A surprising number of American CEOs come from humble backgrounds. It's a long way to the top, but they're fast climbers.

For example, Bill Martin of Phillips Petroleum (who is discussed at length in Chapter 6) was the son of a Dust-Bowl-era grain warehouseman in Oklahoma; Martin's successor, Bill Douce, was the offspring of a rural Kansas druggist; Dave Roderick of USX was a postman's son, while his colleagues Bill Roesch and Al Hillegas were sons of steelworkers; Ron Compton of Aetna was born in Depression-era South Chicago.

BILL DOUCE OF PHILLIPS AND HIS NOTEBOOK

Bill Douce is an apostle of self-reliance. He capped off his superb career at Phillips by fighting off a hostile takeover attempt by the legendary T. Boone Pickens, Jr. One of Douce's colleagues from his early days at Phillips recalled that the future chairman seemed unpromising as a young engineer.

"Bill Douce" he said, "didn't know anything when he came to Phillips. But," he adds, "he was a very curious soul. Everywhere he went in Phillips, he used to carry a notebook.

When somebody would tell him something, he'd write it down."

VIGOROUS OPTIMISM

As an executive and as a communicator, Douce was totally relentless. He sometimes acted as if any problem in life could be overcome through the force of will. In public forums, his favorite phrase about any business, product, or market was "We're optimistic about [it]." His favorite word was "vigorous," as in "We're making vigorous efforts to improve the profitability of our chemicals business."

In communications, he was a perfectionist. He was always trying to make written and oral statements better. One time he called me up at 7 A.M. to come to his house to make changes on a press release. I told him I was baby-sitting for a young daughter and that I'd have to get somebody to watch her. He said, "Bring her along; Willy [his wife] can watch her." I brought my daughter along, and Mrs. Douce took her swimming while Bill and I worked on the release.

Bill Douce (and Willy!) weren't people who worried about corporate and social protocol. Douce was willing to do whatever it took to make improvements that would reflect favorably on Phillips' business and management.

In my dealings with Douce and other CEOs, I've sometimes been reminded of a statement by Aristotle: "All men desire by nature to *know*." The CEOs I've worked with are consumed by curiosity. They want to know *everything* about their organizations; they want to gather all the information and gain all the skills that will advance their careers.

These individuals don't learn to communicate for its own sake. They want to learn to make presentations because it will help them get ahead. They're the kind of people who will work a 60-hour week at the same time they're taking a night-school course in Public Speaking. Their motto could be: "Do it *well* the first time . . . but do it *better* the next time."

THE CEOS AS THEIR OWN (AND SOMETIMES ONLY) CRITICS

The best of the CEOs are their own toughest critics. They also seek out criticism from others. For example, early in my business career I worked on a speech with Bill Martin, Douce's predecessor. Martin was a "central casting" CEO, tall, silver-haired, a former All-American basketball player.

The first time I sat down alone with him, he mentioned he was leaving shortly for a business meeting in Florida. I didn't know enough about the business to say anything intelligent, so I made a lamebrained comment that "you'll probably get some nice weather down there."

Martin, who wasn't exactly heading to Florida for a suntan, looked at me as if I'd just announced I'd seen a flying saucer. I made a serious mental note: "This man does *not* engage in small talk."

On a subsequent occasion, I worked with him on a major speech he was to give in Houston. We flew down together, and the words he spoke to me consisted of the following: "I'm going to take a nap." As he did so, I made another mental note: "This man wants me to keep my mouth shut."

FEAR AND TREMBLING AT 30,000 FEET

He delivered the speech and as the plane rose to take us back to Oklahoma, he peered at me and asked (innocently, I thought): "Well, how did I do?"

My mother didn't bring up any fools, so I immediately said, "You were *great*, boss."

He glowered and said, "I don't need *that.*"

THE TRUTH MAY SET US FREE . . .
BUT FICTION IS EASIER

His point was that sycophantic praise—in those days, my stock in trade—would not help him. How was he to improve without a candid assessment of his performance? He wanted specific information about what he'd done right and, even more important, about where he'd fallen short. In other words, this man, whose weekly paycheck exceeded my yearly wages, wanted my candid views of how he'd delivered his presentation.

At that moment, I remembered an old saying: "When all else fails, try the truth." I then did something I would do at least 100 other times in my career: I gave an honest evaluation of his performance, for which he was grateful.

The best CEOs never think they are good enough; there is always more to learn, always skills to sharpen, always a performance they can improve upon.

In fact, it is "lonely at the top." Many people are cowed by the power of top executives and fear the consequences of being the bearers of bad news. Robert J. Buckley, former CEO of Allegheny International, once said after he'd been brutally (and, in my view, unfairly) cast aside: "I saw dozens of people in my last months at the company. I wish more than a handful had done me the courtesy of telling me the truth."

DON'T ASK THE MIRROR ON THE WALL; ASK THE VIDEOTAPE

Given the difficulty of getting good "feedback," many executives rely on technology. Ron Compton of Aetna rehearsed his performances regularly on videotape, so he could make improvements. Acknowledging the unerring eye of the visual medium, he said, "If you're not good on TV, you're not any good."

A WOMAN WHO WOULD NOT TAKE 'NO' FOR AN ANSWER

One corporate vice president who's in charge of human resources uses both videotapes and audio tapes to analyze her communications. She says, "I learned from the tapes that I had a bad case of the 'ahs' and 'ums.' I've worked on this and I think those 'gremlins' are gone."

She illustrates the point that speaking ability is not inherited; it's earned through effort. When she became a vice president, her communication experience consisted mainly of one-on-one conversations. Suddenly, she was called upon to give major speeches before large, sometimes skeptical, audiences. And she was nervous about it.

She worked with a professional speech writer to get her message down on paper in a style with which she was comfortable. She rehearsed with a speech coach. She taped her delivery and analyzed it with a critical eye. She dropped everything unessential from her schedule so she could immerse herself in her subject matter.

They Didn't Laugh When She Stood Up at the Lectern

The result? She went on stage and made an outstanding speech. It was heartfelt, provocative, and so well-rehearsed that the delivery was smooth and nearly "effortless." (With presentations as with much in life, the more effort that goes into a project, the more effortless it seems.)

GE'S JACK WELCH: A CLASSIC (AND CLASSY) OVERACHIEVER

In this effort, top executives sometimes give new meaning to the phrase "making a virtue out of necessity." One example is Jack Welch, CEO of General Electric. He is one of the classic overachievers who make up such a large part of the CEO ranks.

They Don't Only Hold Bake-offs at Pillsbury

The offspring of a railroad conductor, Welch was the winner of what was perhaps the greatest "bake off" in American corporate history: the four-man battle for the chairmanship of GE. Welch is a highly regarded, if controversial, business manager and strategist.

He's also much admired as a business communicator, which is surprising at first glance. Why? Because when Welch gets excited, he stammers.

When I saw and heard him on a videotape, speaking to Harvard Business School students, it was at first almost embarrassing; the stammer was that noticeable. As the tape went on, however, my response changed. Welch continued to stammer, but this speech defect somehow became progressively less significant. The clarity of his message, coupled with his credibility and conviction, made the speech deficiency almost irrelevant.

The experience reminded me of watching Jim Abbot, pitcher for the California Angels. He was born without a right hand. He pitches left-handed, and has developed a technique for fielding and throwing with his left hand. When Abbot first came to the major leagues, all people could see was his deformed hand. Now, announcers and spectators alike don't even see Abbot's disability. He has transcended it.

So it is with Jack Welch. Like Jim Abbot, he refused to give in to a defect. He made himself an effective communicator when a lesser person might have retreated into silence.

The greatest secret of the CEOs is that a passion for self-improvement is the key to their success.

Many people "um" and "ah" their way through life. They don't have a conception of what kind of speakers they want to be; they don't pinpoint their communication weaknesses—if they are even aware of such deficiencies—and they don't believe they can overcome their shortcomings. They go through life the way they began, inarticulate and ineffective.

PEBBLES IN THE MOUTH . . . OR "ROCKS IN THE HEAD"?

The Greek orator Demosthenes supposedly practiced his craft by speaking with pebbles in his mouth. For those who don't believe they can become more effective speakers, it's not a case of pebbles in the mouth, but of rocks in the head.

Points to Remember:

- Believe you can become a good communicator and you can ultimately achieve it.
- The principles in this book will come alive when you apply them to real-life situations.
- Seek out constructive criticism of your presentations.
- Find out your weaknesses, and turn them into strengths.

3

SELF-ANALYSIS: FINDING OUT WHAT'S BROKEN AND FIXING IT

The first step in learning to communicate better is to become our own best critics. It entails taking a careful look at how we deliver information: seeing and hearing our presentations as others do. If we don't like what we see and hear, then we can change it. Using audio and video tapes, we can see the results of our efforts to improve.

YOU CAN'T FIX IT IF YOU DON'T KNOW WHAT'S BROKEN

Remember the hapless golfer at the driving range? He grips the club so tightly that the veins pop out on his arms; he swings too fast, losing his rhythm and jerking up his head when it should be steady and focused on the ball. The result? The ball either trickles off the tee, or it flies wildly to the left or right.

DON'T HAVE A COW . . . HAVE A GOOD LOOK AT YOURSELF

Why does our inept golfer make these mistakes? Why doesn't he make the adjustments necessary to improve his game? The answer is, he's unaware of his faults. He doesn't see himself as we see him. He may even think his golf swing looks like that of former U.S. Open champion Scott Simpson. Actually, his pitiful efforts are more reminiscent of *Bart* Simpson.

WHO'S THAT STRANGE PERSON INHABITING MY VOICE?

Unfortunately, that's also the case with most would-be communicators. Doubt it? Just recall the first time you heard yourself speaking on a tape recorder. For most people, the experience is like hearing a fingernail scrape across a chalkboard.

At first, we think there must be something wrong with the recorder. Surely this vaguely familiar voice couldn't be ours, with its disconnected thoughts and repetitions, its lack of emphasis, its interminable pauses and embarrassing silences, its nervous interjections of various verbal superfluities, including "y'knows" and "uhs."

It's almost enough to make one take a vow of silence.

AN ALTERNATIVE TO MONASTICISM

However, unless there's a Trappist monastery in your future, you'll find it more helpful to use the tape recorder (audio first, then video) as an ally. Through the phenomenon of electronic tape, you can become a spectator in your own life. By seeing and hearing yourself speak, you can find out what's right with your material and your delivery—and what's wrong. Used correctly, the recorder can point the way to improvements in your presentations.

VISUALIZATION

There's one step to take before you capture yourself on videotape. You should use a technique the psychologists call "visualization." Specifically, you should rely on your imagination to visualize yourself making an excellent presentation in front of an audience.

Imagine yourself speaking concisely, clearly, and convincingly. Imagine yourself delivering a well-organized message on an important subject. Imagine the audience becoming more and more intent on listening to your remarks.

In your visualization, try to imagine the situation in as much detail as possible. What are you wearing? How do you look? Are you standing at a podium, or using a lectern? How many people are there in the audience? Who are they (the general public? people from your company or organization?) What is your subject matter? What words are you using to "sell" the audience on the rightness of your views? Are you speaking from a prepared text or from notes? How are you managing to capture the audience's interest? What variations of tone and emphasis are you using?

Some people might think visualization is a strange process. But this exercise is important. If we're to analyze our current performance as presenters, we need some framework for evaluation. We need to know how we want to look and act in front of an audience, and we need a conception of what response we want to evoke from the audience.

Visualization is the same process we see professional athletes using. For example, before world-class jumpers try to clear the bar, they visualize every aspect of their run and leap. It's a basic psychological principle: Before we can *achieve* something, we first have to *conceive* how it can be done, and then we have to *believe* we can do it.

FROM THE IDEAL TO "REEL"

When you've visualized how you look giving an outstanding presentation, then you're ready to move from the *ideal* to the *reel* (of videotape or audiotape). You're ready to see and hear how your actual performances differ from your visualization, the performance in your "mind's eye."

FIND OUT THE TALE THE TAPE TELLS

The next time you participate in a business or civic meeting, capture your performance on tape. Also, review any taped messages that you may already have. You may have more of these old tapes than you think. They might include everything from the toast you gave at Cousin Harry's wedding to your answering-machine greeting. Any tape you have of yourself speaking is fair game.

GIVE YOURSELF A TOUGH REVIEW

Then, listen to yourself with something approaching cold objectivity. Go through the tapes several times. Compare what you hear and see with what you visualized yourself doing. Put yourself in the role of an unsparing critic, writing down what's good and what's bad about your performance.

As you listen, ask yourself repeatedly: Is this person's message an interesting one? Is it expressed audibly and compellingly? Look for the unconscious repetition of words and phrases (such as, "as I said" or "to make a long story short"). And don't avoid the ultimate question: would I buy a used car from this person? That is, do you sound sincere, credible? If not, why not?

The following list of criteria will give you a systematic way in which to proceed.

SIX CRITERIA IN SEARCH
OF A GOOD SPEAKER

Here are six criteria you can use to evaluate your tapes (but don't hesitate to add your own standards of judgment):

- First, determine whether your message has a "call to action," a request for the audience to *do something*;

- Second, see if your comments systematically support your call to action;

- Third, check the audibility of your statement, making sure the audience can hear what you're proposing;

- Fourth, make sure you choose the words you use based on whether they're appropriate to the circumstances and easy to understand;

- Fifth, focus on the variation in your voice, making sure you emphasize key words and phrases, thus avoiding a monotone;

- Sixth, identify any verbal "tics" you may have, sounds such as "ah" or "um" and superfluous words such as "y'know" or "y'hear."

When you use videotape, add two more criteria: First, is your "body language" (your gestures and physical movements/demeanor) in keeping with your message? Second, do you speak to the audience, or do you bury your head in your notes or text?

Let's look at these points one at a time.

IF YOUR REMARKS DON'T HAVE A POINT, SHARPEN THEM

Criterion #1: The Call to Action. Your recorded comments should have a call to action, a request for the audience to act in response to your remarks.

At this point, you may be saying, "Hey, play fair. How can comments I make at a meeting—or to take an extreme example, my message on an answering machine—have a call to action?" (Does an answering machine message have a call to action? If it's a good one, it certainly does. It goes this way: *"So that I can return your call, please leave your name, phone number, the time you called, and a message."* The highlighted words are the request for the caller to act.)

If your tape is a recording of a business meeting, for example, you might argue that you didn't intend that your comments produce a specific result. *That's not your point;*

instead, it's your problem. In making any comments in public, we shouldn't just say whatever comes into our heads, letting our words flow out in a stream of consciousness. We want them to have direction and purpose. We want them to produce a result. If not, why speak at all?

WARM UP YOUR MEETINGS
BY NOT GOING IN "COLD"

Many formal and informal get-togethers turn into aimless conversational free-for-alls. Why? Because they don't have a theme, a guiding principle, a specific purpose. Of course it's hard for many people to think on their feet—or, at a meeting, "to think on their seat." So the answer is to have a clear idea of what you're going to say before the session begins.

DON'T SLAM DOWN THAT PHONE!

Criterion #2: Support your call to action with specific points. For example, take the answering-machine illustration. You don't want callers to utter silent (or not-so-silent) curses about modern technology and answering machines and hang up. You want them to leave messages. You can encourage this action by saying something like the following: "I'm sorry I'm not available to answer your call" (that is, I'm not just using this infernal machine to screen out calls I don't want to answer).

You might even add a sentence that says, "Your call is important to me" (or better, "I'm glad you called, and I'm sorry I missed speaking directly to you"). This tends to humanize what is basically a mechanical phenomenon. It tends to minimize the caller's frustration at not getting a live human voice.

Perhaps you might precede your call to action with these words: "I promise to get back to you as soon as possible." This gives callers a reason to leave their names, phone numbers, and a short message. (Don't ask them to leave a long message, or they won't bother to leave one at all.)

In other words, every word in your recorded statement should support the call to action. *Your recorded message will have been brief, less than 30 seconds. But it will have fulfilled all the basic elements of a strong presentation: a call to action preceded by logical points supporting that call.*

WHAT IS THE SOUND OF ONE HAND CLAPPING?

It's *silence*, which may be what you hear if your audiences can't hear your presentations.

Criterion #3: Speak up. You've got a problem if the voice on the tape sounds like either (1) Marlon Brando rasping away in the later scenes from *The Godfather, Part II*, or (2) baby birds chirping quietly so as not to wake their parents. When some people speak in public, they sometimes act as if they believe the following proposition: If they can't hear us, they can't take issue with us.

NEXT DICTUM: CHECK YOUR DICTION AND PRONUNCIATION

Criterion #4: Use words carefully. Make sure you use words that are right for the circumstances and that they're understandable to your audience.

Guys, Did You Hear the One about the Traveling Salesman?

In terms of *diction*, you should use words that are appropriate to the setting. Don't be overly formal at a meeting of your bowling group. Don't be overly colloquial if you're speaking in front of the senior management of your company. Avoid jargon whenever possible, especially when you're addressing an audience not familiar with your shop talk. Finally, refrain from off-color language unless you're giving a presentation in a locker room.

As for pronunciation, this mainly becomes an issue if you have a regional or local accent that may be unfamiliar to your listeners. In making presentations, make an extra effort to pronounce your words so they're intelligible. (But don't overpronounce, as with words like "often" (pronounced "offen," with the "t" remaining silent).

When Shakespeare's Polonius said, "Speak the words trippingly on the tongue," he may have been trite, but he also was right. Words should be pronounced clearly, but without an exaggerated "correctness" that makes your statements seem artificial.

"I Won't To Be Alone"

(On regional pronunciation: When the author moved to the Deep South in the 1970s, his young children quickly adopted a "Southern pronunciation." The oldest child, born and brought up in upstate New York, was reviewing her spelling with us one night and said the word "won't," which she then spelled w-a-n-t. We corrected her, "won't, spelled w-o-n-apostrophe-t." She said, "No, w-a-n-t." We asked her to use the word in a sentence. She did: "I wont to go to the sto-ah to buy some candy.")

Say It This Time with Feeling

Criterion #5: *Avoid speaking in a monotone.* Vary the pitch and emphasis of your voice. Unfortunately, most of us fall into a "natural monotone." The tape will tell the tale. If the voice on your tape sounds like the heart monitor of a patient who's recently joined the dearly departed, you have to make some changes. The changes will not be easy, because monotonous speech is a hard habit to break.

Nouns and Verbs? Hit 'em Hard and Often

When you're speaking, put emphasis on the key words, primarily the nouns and verbs. Make the concluding words and phrases in your sentences the important ones, to emphasize the natural rise in voice pitch and emphasis.

For example, suppose you say: "The Japanese are America's toughest competitors, at least in my opinion." The last thing your audience hears is "at least in my opinion," which is not what you want to emphasize. If you want to stress "the Japanese," say: "America's toughest competitors are the Japanese." (Leave out the "in my opinion," which adds nothing.) If you want to highlight the competitive factor, say: "The Japanese are America's toughest competitors." If your statements lack punch, this kind of exercise will help you.

If you're reading from a prepared text, you should make sure the key words in every sentence are at the end. In addition, underline the most significant words in each paragraph. For the most important words in your statement, underline them twice. I used these two techniques with a top executive at USX (formerly U.S. Steel). After he spoke, several people noted how "much more decisive" the executive sounded. In fact, "decisiveness" in speech is largely a matter of syntax, of word order.

For example, if you're terminating your employment and conveying the fact to the boss, you might put it this way: "Take this job and shove it." (However, don't expect a favorable letter of reference.)

And Now We'll Have . . . . an Annoying Pause

Criterion #6: Avoid distracting verbal habits. Any public comments you make should be free of annoying distractions. Ferret out any "verbal tics" you might have and eradicate them. Verbal tics are habits, like repetitions of our old friends "um" and "ah," or phrases like "y'know" and "as I said." Other defects that will keep you out of the Oratorical Hall of Fame include excessive throat clearing and overly long pauses between statements.

. . . AND TWO OTHER CRITERIA FOR VIDEOTAPE

By using videotape, we can not only hear how we sound, but see how we look. Video zeroes in on speakers, accentuating positive and negative elements of their presentation. Overall, it supplements in important ways the knowledge we can gain from audiotapes. Here are two criteria for evaluating your appearance on videotape.

Video: The Finger in the Eye Is a Real Show-stopper

Video Criterion #1: Use videotape to identify gestures that detract from presentations. These include a variety of habits: excessive arm-waving, tie-straightening, leaning to one side or the other, slouching—any activity that calls attention to itself. Of course, appropriate gestures can add emphasis to a presentation. But you want to avoid actions that distract the audience—and detract from your remarks.

For example, I recently saw a supposedly media-wise individual gesturing with both hands in front of his face. The two-dimensional perspective of television made it appear he was in danger of sticking his fingers in his eye or nose. As you might guess, it was hard to concentrate on his message.

Video Criterion #2: Speak to your audience, not to your text or notes. As I've suggested, there's a simple answer to the problem of the downcast eyes: Choose a subject you believe in passionately. That way you'll want to look your listeners in the eye as you share your message with them.

HERE WE WANTED DEMOSTHENES, BUT WE GOT INSTEAD: DISORGANIZATION, DIGRESSIONS, AND DEVIATIONS FROM THE IDEAL

Hearing and seeing ourselves on tape can be a humbling experience. We'll stumble . . . digress . . . repeat ourselves. We may have more "ahs" than a throat doctor's office. We'll demonstrate the logic not of Aristotle, but of Casey Stengel. At our worse, we'll sound less like Demosthenes than like Donald Duck.

A CASE STUDY OF A TELEVISION "PERSONALITY"

When we've completed our video self-analysis, what might it look like? Let's take a real-life analysis I did of a young newswoman at the only commercial TV station, WCAX, in my home state of Vermont. The young journalists at this station are not looking to spend the rest of their lives on the shores of Lake Champlain. They're learning their trade, and when they go to sleep at night they have visions of "plum" assignments in New York, Chicago, or Los Angeles.

Bridget Barry is the "substitute" anchor at WCAX. She's fresh, natural, personable, and intelligent. She should have a good future in television. But if we were to measure her against the ideal news presenter, what points in her delivery could be improved?

First, her "clip-on" microphone on her blouse or sweater sometimes looks something like a black bug. It's distracting. (The national news anchors also use clip-on microphones, but they hide them in the folds of dark clothing.)

Second, like all anchors, Ms. Barry uses a Tele-Prompter. This device allows a presenter to use a prepared text while appearing to speak directly to the audience. In Barry's case, she squints at the TelePrompter as she reads. This may reflect a vision problem or perhaps a too-intense effort not to make a mistake. By making the audience aware of the prompter, however, she runs counter to its purpose: making presentations seem spontaneous.

Third, pacing. She sometimes reads too fast, which can be a sign of nervousness. At the same time, she tends to overpronounce words, for example, the "g" at the end of "ing" words, which is silent in conversational speech. Overall, her pacing is not as calculating as the network people; she lacks those little pauses between selected words and phrases that add drama to a presentation.

Ms. Barry has a beautiful smile, but we rarely get to see it—except when she's kibitzing with the weatherman. She's generally so intent on reading the news that she tends to go into something of a trance.

In other words, she's not a Diane Sawyer, a Connie Chung, or a Jane Pauley. But neither were they when they started. In fact, when we look at early clips of today's news "stars," Ms. Barry looks pretty good in comparison. What differentiates the national news persons from the local hopefuls is practice, experience, and a passion for self-improvement.

Television Accentuates Traits

As this short analysis of one television personality demonstrates, video can be a difficult medium. It tends to accentuate things that would go unnoticed away from the visual medium. Mispronunciations leap out at us. Short pauses in speech can seem to last forever. Unpowdered noses and foreheads reflect like the sun on a mirror.

Why Can't We Be Like They Are (Perfect in Every Way)?

We look at the television anchors on the network news, and we wonder: How can they sound so articulate and polished? Why are they never at a loss for words? How can they talk to 10 million people with the ease of someone chatting to us at the grocery store?

Why Can't We All Sound Like Tom Brokaw?

I'll tell you a secret: we can sound like Tom Brokaw (or Peter Jennings, or Diane Sawyer, or Connie Chung, or like our favorite CEO). We can do so if we recognize that these people are masters of illusion. They are experts at giving the impression of naturalness and spontaneity.

Actually, there's nothing spontaneous about most network news presentations. Everything from the theme song to the closing remarks is scripted ahead of time. The news anchors and their writers put everything on a TelePrompter and then read the words to us. The news anchor's artistry lies in making a scripted presentation sound as natural as the leaves appearing on the trees.

LEAVE NOTHING TO CHANCE

One rule should govern all important presentations— from a meeting with your boss to an address to your trade association: The more important your remarks, the more time you should put into preparing them. Don't ever go into an important meeting without knowing what you're going to say and how you're going to say it.

Make It Easy on Yourself: Forget About Spontaneity

In public communications, the effort to be spontaneous puts pressure on a speaker. Why? Because speech is a window not only to the mind, but to the emotions. In purely "spontaneous speech," all our anxieties, uncertainties, and frustrations are waiting to pop out. (That's why Freudian analysts valued "free association," which is nothing more than the flow of speech unfiltered by the conscious mind.)

For example, during T. Boone Pickens' attempted takeover of Gulf Corporation, he made a lot of that company's executives angry. One of them was a Gulf executive vice president. When *The New York Times* asked him what Gulf's strategy was for dealing with Pickens, he replied, "We're going to kick him in the b——."

When asked what he thought of Citibank CEO Walter Wriston for giving Pickens a line of credit usable in the Gulf takeover, the Gulf executive noted he was scheduled to play tennis with Wriston and said that perhaps he would "shove the racket down that little b——'s throat."

Needless to say, Wall Street did not regard these remarks as the considered judgments of a secure and confident company. Gulf was soon acquired by Standard Oil of California.

The Gulf executive's comments were a case of responding with his heart rather than with his head. (I agreed then—and agree now—with his characterizations of corporate raider Pickens and corporate windbag Wriston.) However, better preparation would have led to better (or at least, more politic) answers to the press.

SOMETIMES YOU SHOULD TALK INTO THE MICROPHONE; SOMETIMES YOU SHOULD JUST SMILE AT IT

Just because there's a microphone or lectern in front of you is no reason to start talking. If you haven't thought carefully about what you want to say, it's best to defer your comments. It's sometimes best to smile and say, "I don't have anything to say right now, but when I do, you'll be the first to hear about it."

Would You Hire This Man?

We see this point illustrated in a statement by Billy Sullivan, then general manager of the New England Patriots, at the time the worst team in professional football. A reporter asked Sullivan if he was about to be fired—a query akin to asking if the nights are cold in Iceland.

Sullivan's response was: "I think . . . ah . . . that I . . . ah . . . have things . . . ah . . . to add . . . ah . . . to this . . . ah . . . organization."

Billy Sullivan sounded like a man about to be fired, and he "resigned" shortly thereafter.

If You Have 'em by the Throat, Their Hearts and Minds Are Sure to Follow

Contrast Sullivan's indecisiveness with the statement later the same day by another New England sportsman. Responding to a question by his former teammate, Bob Cousy, Tom Heinsohn talked about how a team should avoid letting down against an inferior opponent.

Heinsohn said, "Take 'em seriously. Play hard early. Keep your foot on their throat."

Heinsohn's style in this statement exemplifies an approach that's characteristic of American CEOs and their counterparts in government and the military. I call it "blunt eloquence." It's simple, concise, and straightforward.

It's probably also too good to be spontaneous. It sounds very much as if Heinsohn had the answer before Cousy asked the question. In contrast, Billy Sullivan probably still doesn't have the answer to the question the reporter asked him.

The problem with relying on spontaneity is that it makes the speaker a hostage to circumstances, to chance. In this regard, consider the response of Louis Pasteur when a questioner asked him what role luck played in scientific discoveries. Pasteur said, "Chance favors the prepared mind." In other words, good luck results from adequate preparation.

Points to Remember:

- Listen to yourself on audio- and videotape to make your own objective evaluation of your presentations.

- Know ahead of time exactly what you want to say and how you want to say it.

- Put a lot of preparation into your presentations, and the results will show it. If you "wing it," there's a high potential for a crash landing.

4

THE CEOS
AND "BLUNT ELOQUENCE":
THE DIRECT APPROACH

The most effective statements in the best presentations are short, meaningful, and memorable. Examples would be Patrick Henry's "Give me liberty or give me death"; Calvin Coolidge's "I do not choose to run"; Douglas MacArthur's "Old soldiers never die"; and John F. Kennedy's "I am a Berliner." They are statements so brief that they seem blunt. But they are so memorable and evocative that they're also eloquent.

At their best, top leaders in business, government, and the military speak with this "blunt eloquence." Their statements are concise, clear, and confident.

WAS ANYONE AWAKE AT THE END?
A STATEMENT THAT'S NEITHER BLUNT
NOR ELOQUENT

Unfortunately, a lot of speakers are neither blunt nor eloquent. The following statements are from a telephone industry spokesperson supporting a Department of Justice recommendation to allow the regional telephone companies to offer long-distance service in competition with companies AT&T, MCI, and Sprint.

Before getting to my assigned topic, the manufacturing issue, I'd like to beg your indulgence while I touch briefly on the D(epartment) O(f) J(ustice) proposal regarding inter-city competition.

The bottom line of that D(epartment) O(f) J(ustice) rec-ommendation is that the Bell Regionals should be permit-ted to provide a full range of long-distance services only after the states have eliminated all legal and regulatory barriers to competition in the local exchange market.

The recommendation is perfect, theoretically, but un-tenable as a practical matter.

State regulators will not move quickly to unravel the franchise obligations of the regional telephone operating companies.

The political deck is stacked against restructuring the local exchange market moving prices to costs and elimi-nating all the subsidies that now support rates for protected classes of customers.

The speech goes on (and on) in a similar vein. It is a dreadful speech. The speaker was an amiable individual, a good conversationalist fiercely proud of his golf game, his distinguished looks, and his social skills. In formal presen-tations, however, he turned into "Mr. Hyde," purveyor of polysyllables ("untenable . . . theoretically") and phone com-pany jargon ("DOJ"). There are a lot of words in his speech, but the sound of the human voice communicating is absent.

The problems in the speech segment I've quoted start with the absurd reference to an "assigned topic," a term most of us associate with junior high school. Thereafter, the words in the speech bang into each other like bumper cars at an amusement park.

The second sentence/paragraph has 42 words. Reading that many words effectively would require the lung power of a marathon runner. On the audience's part, comprehending that sentence would require the mental capacities of Einstein.

In terms of conversational style, has anyone seriously "begged . . . indulgence" since the age of Queen Victoria?

Also, what's the difference between "intercity competition" (paragraph one) and "long-distance services?" Answer: none. Moreover, why use the word "unravel" in terms of the phone companies' "franchise obligations"? Answer: It seemed like a more significant word than (the more appropriate) "remove."

In addition, what does the speaker mean when he refers to "restructuring the local exchange market"? We have no way of knowing.

Finally, why use the "deck is stacked" cliché in the last paragraph/sentence (of 29 words)? Answer: A resounding cliché was in keeping with the dead phraseology that preceded—and followed—it.

Why would anyone make such a terrible speech? I believe exceptionally bad presentations have their origins in a lack of candor and honesty. Also, the fingerprints of company lawyers are in evidence throughout the speech segment. Their theory? What you say can't be held against you, especially if you don't say anything.

The Art of Speaking at Length Without Saying Anything

The telephone company speech is verbally flabby. It uses too many words to say too little. It relies on endless qualifications which ensure that no one will ever call the speaker to task for anything he says. It uses jargon that ensures those "outside the industry" will not understand the remarks.

There's no sign that the speaker ever looked inside himself. He didn't ask, "What am I really trying to say?" He didn't try to boil down his message to its central points. He didn't make his statements brief enough to say with ease or, at least, with one breath. He didn't try to make his statement decisive and forthright. Thus, the comments come across as hesitant, awkward, and evasive. The audience presumably left with the assumption that the man had something to hide.

BE NOTHING IF NOT DECISIVE

Decisiveness is the key to blunt eloquence. By definition, a true leader is not a bag of airy sentiments. The leader is a man or woman of a few carefully chosen words. When the leader wants to make a point, the audience almost recoils from the impact.

Speech scholar Kathryn Hall Jamieson has described what I call "blunt eloquence" as speech that is "factual, analytical, organized, and impersonal." Blunt eloquence is a style that used to be called (in the prefeminist days) "masculine." Blunt eloquence is, however, an approach used by successful males and females alike.

THE LADY WHO TAUGHT ME A LESSON

I learned several years ago that successful people of both sexes prefer the approach I've called "blunt eloquence." The lesson was provided by a woman who's a successful politician in Pennsylvania. In her abrasive, aggressive approach to politics, she reminds some people of Bella Abzug.

The Pennsylvania woman asked me to write her a speech. I did so. More accurately, I produced an essay—a nice little piece tied together with all the rhetorical and grammatical elements we learned in English 101.

She didn't like the speech. She said it reminded her of "garden club" niceties. "Write me a speech," she said, "that sounds like it came out of the mouth of a corporate executive." She added, "In other words, make it sound like a statement by a grown woman, not by one of the 'girls.' "

She objected especially to my heavy use of "transition" words—"however, therefore, consequently," and so forth—

believing (correctly) those terms made the remarks overly formal. She also disliked my abstract approach to her topic, which she thought (again, correctly) made the remarks sound too philosophical, and thus indecisive. She wanted remarks that were an exercise of will and self-assurance.

Words that Leave an Imprint

Blunt eloquence is verbally aggressive. It's the style we associate with General Norman Schwarzkopf, Lee Iacocca, and General Colin Powell. The latter illustrated the bluntly eloquent approach in a news conference when he was asked what the military's strategy was for dealing with the Iraqi army in Kuwait. Powell said, "We're going *to cut it off*, and then we're going *to kill it*."

Plain Speech as a Wake-Up Call

Powell's statement is one that's designed to get our attention. It does so by using two provocative words: "cut" and "kill."

Suppose Powell answered the question by saying, "Our strategic objective is to interdict the lines of supply and reinforcement of the Iraqi army and then subsequently to defeat it in battle." This is the "cut it off . . . and kill it" statement stripped of its color and evocativeness. The longer version adds words while it drains the statement of its power and effect.

Blunt Eloquence and Forceful Language

Another speaker who takes a verbally aggressive approach to communication is GE's Jack Welch. In one statement, quoted in *Fortune* magazine, he talked about his company's move away from a management style that emphasized control to one stressing counseling, allocating resources, and encouraging thoughts. Welch said, "We're going to win on our *ideas* . . . not by *whips* and *chains*."

The use of the unusual words "whips" and "chains" helps make Welch's statement memorable. Suppose Welch had said, "We're going to win on the quality of our intellectual analyses . . . not by using rigid controls and firm directives?" By so doing, he would have removed the highly memorable images in his statement.

Ron Compton of Aetna used an approach similar to Welch's. Speaking about initiatives he'd launched to shake up Aetna, Compton spoke about them as "conceptual hand grenades." If he'd talked just about "concepts" or "ideas" or "initiatives," his comment would have lost its effectiveness.

Speakers use aggressive images for a simple reason: *Audiences hear such words and phrases.* They realize that audiences *don't* hear the abstractions of everyday language. Presenters who use predictable, "low risk" language don't get through to the people they're trying to reach.

Blunt Eloquence: Less Is More

In fact, in many cases, the more a speaker says, the less the audience will remember. Lincoln's Gettysburg Address lasted less than seven minutes, and his speech remains memorable. The speaker (Edward Everett) who followed Lincoln talked for hours, but who remembers anything he said?

Blunt eloquence is the art of taking dull rhetoric and sharpening the language to make it memorable. As part of that process, we boil down what we want to say to its essence.

Many of the most effective statements made in presentations are statements of seven words or less. They're reminiscent of President Bush's comments on taxes—"Read my lips. No new taxes."—or Reagan's promise to Congress to veto legislation it had vowed to pass—"C'mon, make my day."

Blunt eloquence also manifests itself in rapid-fire sentences. We see this in Rohm & Haas' Larry Wilson's appeal to Latin American nations to embrace free trade: "Protectionism is not the answer. Exports *and* imports are the answer. Mutually beneficial growth is the answer."

Such statements hit the audience the way Rocky Marciano used to hit his opponents—hard, fast, and often. They demonstrate how much meaning a speaker can pack into short, declarative sentences. Also, they show thoughts crafted and polished to maximum effect.

HOW YOU CAN ACHIEVE
BLUNT ELOQUENCE

In presentations, blunt eloquence doesn't "just happen." It's the result of pruning and polishing your thoughts and notes. Here are some steps you can take to sharpen your statements:

Pulverize the Polysyllables

First, try not to use many words with more than two syllables. This is not a plea for anti-intellectualism. Instead, it's a recognition that "big words" tend—by their excessive formality—to weigh down statements. Polysyllables are often hard to pronounce, mainly because we see them in print much more often than we use them in speech.

Charlie Kittrell of Phillips Petroleum loved it when I told him the word "disintermediation" referred to people taking their money out of banks and putting it into stocks, bonds, or mutual funds. Similarly, Jerry McAfee, Gulf CEO, amused audiences by telling them that economists were talking about "supply elasticity of demand." McAfee said the term meant nothing more than "When something costs more, people buy less."

Good Presentations Don't Sound Like Any Graduation Speech You Ever Heard

Second, rely mainly on simple, declarative sentences. These can be subject-verb sentences (I came; I saw; I conquered.), or they can be subject-verb-object sentences: (I came to Peoria; I saw a beautiful woman; I conquered her heart.). Use adverbs and adjectives sparingly.

That Which Should Be Avoided

Stay away from words that complicate—and elongate—your sentences. These words include "that," "which," and "who"—"subordinating conjunctions" in the grammarian's lexicon. Consider the following sentence: "The comptroller, who had earlier decided to take another job, later reconsidered and stayed at the firm." This phrasing demands a high level of attentiveness by the audience, and it sounds overly formal and stuffy.

To make the comment more conversational and understandable, turn it into two sentences. "The comptroller had earlier decided to change jobs. But he later reconsidered and stayed at the firm."

What's true of subordinating conjunctions is doubly true of subordinating adverbs, words like *until, when, since, because, although, if,* and *as if.* These words are too formal for most presentations. Also, they demand that the audience connect ideas in ways that are difficult for listeners.

For example, consider this sentence: Although the tax implications for the project were favorable, real estate conditions finally dictated a decision not to go forward. If this statement is in writing, it can always be reread if it's not understood on first reading.

Sam Won't "Say It Again"

But in a presentation, if we don't hear a statement correctly, there's no second chance. That's why it makes sense to turn the example above into two (colloquial) sentences: Investing in the project might have lowered our taxes. But the current lack of rental clients for real estate caused us to reject the deal. This approach breaks up the ideas into "digestible" chunks, a point listeners will appreciate.

A PRESENTATION THAT EXEMPLIFIES
BLUNT ELOQUENCE

The techniques discussed here will help you in your drive to achieve a simpler, clearer, more decisive style. However, blunt eloquence derives mainly from mental habits. If your mind is muddled, it's hard to keep your comments brief and to the point.

One man whose statements are a model of clarity is Thomas J. ("Tom") Fay, senior vice president of communications at United Technologies Corporation. Fay is an individual known for speaking his mind.

Fay was asked for a statement on the subject of Leadership and Career Development. This is a hard topic for a no-nonsense type like Fay. That's because it's a subject that attracts hot air and clichés the way horse manure attracts flies.

Just the Facts, Man

As Fay tells us, the facts are these: If we really knew how to produce leaders, we'd have more of them around. As for "career development," if we truly valued it, we wouldn't have put low-status individuals in charge of it.

The challenge for Fay was to make something of the topic. The following is the statement he developed.

Leadership and Career Development
Thomas J. Fay
Senior Vice President, Communications
United Technologies

Terms like career development or leadership development can encourage wrong thinking.

Career development is mainly self-development. No one is "developed" as a leader or manager or professional. They develop themselves. They may require a (corporate) structure that's open to development.

It's nice to work for a boss who sponsors your development. It's also nice to have lots of resources to aid in your development, but it's like leading the proverbial horse to water. Once you've got him there, he may or may not drink.

You have to look at all development as a function of energy, dedication, ambition, and intelligence. In general, people who want to get ahead—who wish to develop— can do so under almost any circumstances, and people who are not so inclined will not be developed under any circumstances.

What a corporation can do—and basically all that it can do—is offer opportunities, chart courses, measure performance, and open doors.

It's still up to the individual. Hard work is involved. Luck is involved. Visibility is involved.

I'd be very suspicious of a person who joined a company right after college and progressed smoothly in two-year spans of ever-increasing responsibility to the chairman's office. Life isn't like that.

The war in the Middle East provided examples of leaders at work. President Bush assembled a collection of sometimes unmotivated nations and helped direct them toward a single goal.

General Schwarzkopf is a good example of a different kind of leadership: an intense focus, a clear mission, a marshalling of resources to undertake and complete the mission, patience and steadfastness, and strategic brilliance.

Fay Has Something to Say

Fay's presentation is a good one—short and tart. His remarks are interesting because they skillfully deny the premise underlying the topic: that we know how to develop leaders and managers. In other words, he takes his topic and turns it on its head. He suggests that "developing" leaders consists largely of getting out of their way; he indicates that career development is mainly a matter of an individual's character.

When All Else Fails, Try the Truth

Thus, in terms of content, Fay surprises his audience, which presumably is waiting for the pitter-patter of tiny platitudes. At the same time, however, he confirms a view the audience probably holds: that phrases like "career development" are generally airy abstractions.

Tom Fay's statement is very much in character. He is a blunt and straightforward man and a man of relatively few words. When I worked for him at Aetna, I noticed that he wrote few memos, and those he did write contained fewer words, and more sense, than anyone else's. He worried over every word in those memos. He had a passion for getting his point across in just the right way.

The Word Made Flesh

Fay's statement on leadership is the incarnation of blunt eloquence. For example, look at the number of short, punchy sentences, many of them six words or less: Career development is mainly self-development; They develop themselves; Life isn't like that; Hard work is involved. Luck is involved. Visibility is involved.

Such sentences result from rigorous thought and a passion for simplicity and clarity. (Fay probably would respond that his incisive statements "are the result of revising cumbersome statements and cutting out unnecessary words.")

The best writing and the best speaking are a lot like the purest diamonds. They're the result of intense pressure (mental in one case, physical in the other) and ceaseless polishing.

Keep the Nouns and Verbs, Discard the Rest

Another element of blunt eloquence is the emphasis on nouns and verbs. Look at the section of Fay's statement that talks about what a corporation can do for its people. He says it can "offer opportunities, chart courses, measure perform- ance, and open doors." In every case, we have a verb followed by a noun. For the "bluntly eloquent," nouns are specific, and verbs tell what the object did or, more rarely, what was done to it. Adjectives are general—abstract—while nouns relate to specific persons, places, and things.

Of Punchy Lines and Punching Bags

As Fay's comments illustrate, blunt eloquence resem- bles the actions of a skilled boxer. At times, the words and sentences come without an almost metronomic quality (Hard work . . . luck . . . visibility). One verbal blow follows another, all of them delivered with intensity and feeling. It's some- thing like reading a novel by Ernest Hemingway.

But as all good boxers know, a knockout punch has to be set up. For example, look at the way Fay gives us an unusually (for him) long sentence: "I'd be very suspicious of a person who joined a company right after college and progressed smoothly in two-year spans of ever-increasing responsibility to the chairman's office." He follows this statement with the verbal equivalent of a short right hook: "Life isn't like that."

Question: Are They Sorry They Asked Him?

One might fault Fay's statement for not having an explicit call to action, but in this case his point was to stimulate thought rather than action. We can see his com- ments as answering a specific question: "What should the corporation do about leadership development and career development?" His answer: "Stop wasting time, money, and words on them; instead, hire good people; then create an environment where they can achieve their potential and become leaders."

KEEP IT SIMPLE

Blunt eloquence is speech that results from clear thinking and simple language. When you're preparing a presentation, ask yourself at the end of every paragraph: What am I really trying to say? Is there an easier, clearer, better way to express my point?

Asking these questions will help you find the heart of your message, the essence of what you want to say.

Simplicity Is the Best Policy

"An entirely new school of speaking has sprung up since the Civil War. In keeping with the spirit of the times, it is as direct as a telegram. . . . A modern audience, whether it is fifteen people at a business conference or a thousand people under a tent, wants the speaker to talk just as directly as he would in a chat, and in the same general manner that he would employ in speaking to them in conversation." (Dale Carnegie, *Public Speaking,* 1926)

The simple, direct style of communication is clearly the best approach. However, clarity in expression is rare in the military, government, education, and business.

Unfortunately, we learn the unclear modes of expression in school, particularly in high school and college. Doubt it? Have you ever met a child who couldn't get across the point that he or she was hungry? Cold? Tired? Or who couldn't tell you "where it hurts"? It's only as we grow older that we begin to obfuscate our messages.

**FRANK PACETTA: A TOUGH TALKER
LOOKS FOR EXAMPLES OF BLUNT ELOQUENCE
AND EMULATES THEM**

Where you find a speaker using "blunt eloquence," you'll find someone speaking clearly. You'll also generally find a successful individual. For example, when I was writing this chapter, I read an article in *The Wall Street Journal* about Frank Pacetta, a very successful salesman and manager for Xerox. The *Journal* describes him as "a taskmaster who evokes both love and fear in his troops."

How does Pacetta talk? Regarding his management style, he says, "I'll recognize you lavishly, but I expect you to pay the rent. If you don't, you'll pay the consequences." Describing his own sales abilities, Pacetta is not modest, saying, "I could sell snow to an Eskimo."

Pacetta also demonstrates the aggressive diction characteristic of blunt eloquence. Of sales, he says, "It's lonely, and it's a war." About employees who perform poorly, he observes, "If someone is just going through the motions, I have no trouble pulling the trigger."

Colin Powell, Tom Fay, Frank Pacetta, Norman Schwarzkopf, Jack Welch, and the others I've mentioned have these points in common: They're all successful, and they all express themselves with blunt eloquence. The success and the language go together—for them and for you.

Points to Remember:

- Avoid "verbal flab," excess words and complicated sentences.
- Make your statements short, meaningful, and memorable.
- Achieve blunt eloquence by making each of your statements decisive and incisive.
- Use "aggressive" language to get an audience's attention.

5

MEMORABLE
PRESENTATIONS:
HOW THEY GET THAT WAY

Skilled presenters make their presentations memorable by relying on the full resources of the language. They use grown-up versions of a memory device found in nursery rhymes: repetition of sounds, words, and phrases.

WORDS WITH A RING TO THEM

It has been said that history is the story of the exploits of political and military leaders. But history is also the story of catchy phrases, many of them shrouded in the mists of time. The nineteenth century spawned many catch phrases: "Fifty-four forty or fight" were once fighting words.

So was the attack on a presidential candidate (and alleged prevaricator) who was characterized by his political enemies as "James G. Blaine, continental liar from the state of Maine." And the anti-immigrant Know-Nothing Party spoke darkly of Roman Catholic and pro-alcohol conspiracies with the phrase "Rum, Romanism, and Rebellion." When Benjamin Harrison, hero of the battle of Tippecanoe, chose Tyler as his presidential running mate, sloganeers came up with "Tippecanoe and Tyler too." The twentieth century chimed in with "I Like Ike" and its lesser-known Democratic counterpart, "Madly for Adlai [Stevenson]."

Beyond political slogans, some things have been said so well that they burn themselves into our memories. These statements include Franklin Roosevelt's "The only thing we have to fear is fear itself"; Churchill's admission that the British people would have to endure, "blood, sweat, toil, and tears" (yes, he used the word *toil*); John Kennedy's "Ask not what your country can do for you. Ask instead what you can do for your country." And George Bush's call for "a kinder, gentler nation."

The examples in the preceding two paragraphs rely on similar sounds or word orders for their effect. Spoken aloud, they seem to echo in our minds. Thus, when sound reinforces substance, we get memorable phrases.

MOST WORDS ARE "WRITTEN ON THE WIND"

In a lifetime, the average person will speak millions of words, few of them memorable. Yet we can take steps to ensure that the important things we have to say do leave an impression.

As you've seen, one way to make an impression is to speak with "blunt eloquence." That approach is "the art of boiling down," of speaking crisply and clearly. It's communicating the essence of what we have to say in simple, forceful language.

It's important to pay attention not only to what we want to say, but to how we say it. Why? Because if we don't, we risk losing our audience. As any presentation proceeds, the audience tends to lose interest in it. Thus, presenters need to make a constant effort to say things that engage their listeners' interest. Getting people to remember our key points means using language in unusual ways.

Use Speech as a "Wake-Up Call"

In other words, speakers need to seed their presentations with "wake-up calls." They need to use fresh language in providing relevant information, examining issues, and defining problems. They need to purge their presentations of stale language: jargon, clichés, and empty abstractions.

Using colorful, effective language helps to reinforce a solid message with a clear call to action. In addition, a presenter's emotional "pitch" conveys commitment to a message.

INTENSITY IS THE KEY

Audiences tune out lines delivered without passion. So it's important that speakers deliver key lines with force and emphasis—with "intensity." Audiences respond to speakers' efforts to get their points across. If the presenter thinks the message deserves a heavy expenditure of energy—a forceful delivery, one tinged with emotion—the audience generally will listen with mental and emotional involvement.

Athletic coaches stress the need for "intensity" in sporting events. They're talking about the need for athletes to sustain their efforts throughout a contest, to try hard, to give their best. Coaches know that when athletes get tired, they become less intense; they start to "go through the motions."

INTENSITY IN ACTION: BOB GATES FIGHTS FOR HIS PROFESSIONAL LIFE

A good example of a speaker showing intensity was CIA Deputy Director Robert Gates in his confirmation hearings (in late 1991) to become director of the Agency. In the early phases of his testimony, Gates was a bland speaker, his comments guarded, his tone monotonous. Later in the hearing, critics came forward with serious charges. They accused him of politicizing the agency's analysis of issues. One detractor accused Gates of intentionally misinforming the President on a major policy question.

No More Mr. Bland Guy

When Gates responded, he spent all day on the witness stand. He was no longer the plodding bureaucrat. His integrity had been questioned, and he was angry. Words came out of his mouth with the intensity of bullets slamming into a target. In his prepared statement, he listed 20 charges critics had made against him. He went through each one, concluding after each discussion: *"That allegation is false."*

Gates testified for an entire day (about as physically demanding as running a marathon) and then returned to the witness chair the next morning. By manifesting a high energy level, he came across to many viewers as a man who had been unfairly accused and wasn't going to take it any more. In fighting for his professional life, he gave every appearance of being a man with the courage of his convictions. This time of his adversity probably was his finest hour.

WHEN THE GOING GETS TOUGH, THE TOUGH GET GOING

It's important that speakers recognize the need to give their best effort throughout a presentation. An audience will pay most attention to speakers at two points: the beginning and the end.

How do you get an audience's attention in the middle of a presentation? You do so by "turning up your intensity level a notch" (as football coaches often say). In fact, an audience's attention is directly proportional to a speaker's intensity. As the presentation goes on, the speaker gets tired as the audience's "attention curve" declines.

It's up the speaker to counteract this phenomenon to keep the audience attentive throughout the presentation. That can be done by giving increasing emphasis to key words and phrases as the speech goes on.

From The Desk Of:
Antonio Giraldi
(310) 858-2924

You can remember to do this by writing messages to yourself in your speech text or notes. Writing the word *intensity* at key points throughout your text will help. So will underlining or **boldfacing** important words and concepts in the text—perhaps with double underlining of key points in the last one third of the remarks. (One of my clients had a "raging red bull" stamp he used to mark crucial concepts in his texts.)

Dramatize Your Main Points—Give Them a "Plot"

Another way to make your presentations memorable is to inject drama into them. This involves careful organization of your material, as well as using voice inflection and timing to emphasize certain points. In other words, it involves your becoming a "ham."

Many otherwise good presentations fail because of a lack of drama. They just "go on and on." There is little or no effort to highlight key ideas, or to heighten the audience's expectations. The flow of information is so steady the presentation begins to sound like a babbling brook. For listeners, the experience is like reading a story without a plot.

The best speakers are good dramatic actors. Think about Billy Graham's sermons. To his rapt listeners, he's not just "talking about" the importance of religion. Instead, he's outlining the struggle that goes on in the individual's soul. He talks about dramatically opposed concepts: faith and disbelief, good and evil, salvation and damnation. He's telling a story the theme of which is: My Kingdom is not of this earth. And the crowds flock by the tens of thousands to hear him.

STUART ALTMAN: THE ECONOMIST AS DRAMATIST

Graham's evangelical religion lends itself to dramatic oratory. But even for presenters with relatively mundane subjects, drama is not only possible, but achievable.

Some time ago, I listened to a speech by Dean Stuart H. Altman of Brandeis University. A slight, diminutive man, Altman's subject was "The Economics of Health Care in the United States." Not the most promising of speech topics, especially for an address delivered at 7:30 P.M. to an audience waiting for dinner.

Altman made the wait worthwhile. His talk was polished and witty. (He said his alma mater, the University of Chicago School of Economics, wouldn't grant candidates a Ph.D. until they had "a religious experience," believing that "the free market" would cure all ills.) One of Altman's themes dealt with how he lost this "faith" as he studied the economics of health care.

Altman discussed how health-care costs had tripled in four decades as a percentage of national spending. He presented this fact as a mystery, which he proceeded to solve. Specifically, he discussed each decade as presenting an economic riddle for health care economists. With oratorical skill, he led the audience slowly but inexorably to each riddle's solution. Listening to Altman speak was something like watching Itzhak Perlman play the violin or Joe DiMaggio play center field.

A SUREFIRE RECIPE FOR INJECTING DRAMA

As I've indicated, audiences don't want mere "information." *They want information that leads somewhere*; they want answers; they want to know what they should do about the information you present (that is, they want a "call to action"). In a Biblical sense, they want the presenter to be Moses, leading them to "the promised land."

One way to do this is to structure your presentation in terms of questions and answers. For example, Altman's talk asked, "What happened in the 1960s to make health care less available to people generally?" (His answer was that insurance companies stopped insuring everyone who applied and started trying to insure only healthy people.)

Don't Spill the Beans; Dole Them Out

In other words, start with a question, and then make the audience wait a few minutes for the answer. Skillful speakers don't just *present information. They withhold information* until the time is right to reveal it. Proceed in that way, and you'll be taking the audience on a journey of discovery. They will join you in finding the answers to your stated or implicit questions. Ultimately, those answers will dictate the course of action you will propose.

HOW ARE PRESENTATIONS LIKE SYMPHONIES AND SEX? (ANSWER: EVERYTHING BUILDS TO A CLIMAX)

Another way of making your presentations more dramatic is to pay attention to syntax, to the way you order your words as well as sentences and paragraphs in the entire presentation.

Presentations should continually build to climaxes. All the points you use in supporting your call to action should be good. But you should save your best material for the final moments of your presentation. End on a high note, which is generally an emotional one.

For example, if you're speaking to a group of shareholders for your company, conclude by telling how the actions you propose are going to increase the value of their shares. If you're delivering a locker-room pep talk to a youth football team, tell them how sweet victory will be.

What's true of entire presentations is true of their smallest elements: words, phrases, and sentences. Construct your sentences so that they end on key words and phrases. Don't say, "This was their finest hour, more or less." Say instead, "This was their finest hour." That is, end on a high note, with a bang rather than with a whimper. (Look again at the previous chapter on "blunt eloquence." You'll note that this type of expression reflects the need to end with key words and phrases, for example, "cut it off . . . kill it".)

THROW OUT THE BATHOS
WITH THE BATH WATER

When you make lists in your presentations, don't proceed from more important elements to less important. Supposedly a Yale student did this during World War I when he said he was enlisting "for God, for country, for Yale." Read the quote aloud; it sounds funny, because the syntax implies that Yale is more important than country or God. The rhetoricians have given this unintentional anticlimax a name: *bathos.*

Tom Fay of United Technologies has a good memory device for recalling the order of climax. He says, "In an ecclesiastical procession, the place of honor is at the end." Remember this the next time you see a Vatican procession with the cardinals preceding the Pope. (In my first draft, I had the previous sentence reading—bathetically—"Remember that the next time you see a Vatican procession with the Pope following the cardinals.")

PERSONAL STORIES

One way to catch an audience's attention is by using personal stories. Most presentations are too *im*personal. They use language that's detached, logical, and analytical. This approach can lose an audience. It can become a case of the bland leading the bored.

On the other hand, personal stories inject an element of the unexpected into presentations. Most formal presentations give us a view of the "public" self, of someone speaking in an official or semiofficial role. We don't expect the self-revelation of the personal story. When we get it, we're surprised, and our attention level rises. We want to hear more.

RON COMPTON'S MARBLES

A skillful use of a personal story occurs in a speech by Ron Compton made to insurance agents representing Aetna. When Compton made this speech, relations between Aetna and its agents were difficult.

Compton began his talk by referring to these contentious issues. Then he referred to "the marble story." He said:

> *I was born and raised on the South Side of Chicago in the Depression. And you learned a lot of things; one was never fight a kid you've never seen. He's probably a foot taller than you are.*
>
> *Another was: when you're fighting with your best friend at recess over whose Aggie marble that is, never, never forget one thing. That it's the kids on the next block that are going to try to beat the hell out of you on the way home.*
>
> *You and I—you and Aetna—are best friends. We're in the same neighborhood. We have the same outlooks. We really have the same goals.*
>
> *And remember: There are kids on the next block. They're the extremist legislators, regulators, and consumer activists who would just as soon beat us up.*

(I received praise from various individuals for writing these lines. My inclination was to accept the praise. But I had to admit that Compton wrote those lines himself.)

His engaging "marble story" accomplishes several things: It breaks down the barriers that separate a top executive from the "hired help"; it establishes the speaker's humanity, making him not only an order giver and policymaker, but a crafty former marbles player; it suggests—without explicitly saying so—that Compton is "street smart," a graduate of the South Chicago sidewalks. Finally, it makes the point that unless the company and the agents hang together, "the kids on the next block" will do them in.

LARRY WILSON AND THE LONELINESS
OF THE LONG-DISTANCE ROWER

Another executive who uses personal stories effectively is Larry Wilson, CEO of Rohm & Haas. Wilson likes to speak about the need for teamwork in business. This is a subject that—in hands other than Wilson's—often leads to predictable comments, even banality.

Wilson, however, gives a fresh perspective to teamwork in a graduation speech he made at a Pennsylvania high school. He said, "When I was in high school, I used to row crew . . . the ultimate *team* sport. A member of a crew has a definite, individual job to do. But the crew wins or loses as a team. A winning boat has every rower pulling together. It minimizes weight . . . and it doesn't carry anybody who's just along for the ride."

Metaphors

Wilson's use of rowing blends personal reference and the technique of metaphor. A metaphor is a comparison of two dissimilar things without using "like" or "as" (which are the words that characterize a particular kind of metaphor known as a simile). In plain English, a metaphor occurs when you call a person, place, or object something it's not, for example, if you say your beloved is a "red, red rose."

Quick, How Is the Federal Government
Like a Fat Boy?

Elizabeth Dichter, an Arizona executive, used metaphor in describing to *Fortune* the great influence the government's Medicare program has on prescription-drug prices. She said, "The government is the fat boy in the canoe. When it leans, everybody else winds up on the same side of the boat."

Jim Lynn of Aetna used a metaphor of a famous historical battle to describe his company's resolve in the face of political criticism. He said, "We have no intention of retreat-

ing into a political Alamo, continually on the defensive . . .
in a deteriorating position."

MORE THAN JUST ANOTHER FISH STORY

Skillful speakers can structure entire presentations
around metaphors. This is what an ITT Educational Services
executive did in a presentation to Caribbean investors and
elected officials. She discussed the role ITT educational
franchises could play in providing jobs and improving telecommunications in the Caribbean nations.

The speaker organized her remarks around an old
saying: "Give someone a fish, and you'll feed them for a day.
Teach them to fish, and you'll feed them for a lifetime." She
added that ITT's educational programs "teach people to fish
in the pool called 'economic opportunity.'"

She wove the "teach/fish" metaphor throughout her
remarks. Her point was that telecommunications links and
a skilled work force were essential to attracting industries.
She concluded by stating that her firm's educational services
offered "the nations of the Caribbean and Central America
the opportunity to fish productively in the high technology
pond of advanced communications."

The metaphor is appropriate, especially given the
Caribbean's historic reliance on fishing. In fact, the metaphor may be the one thing imprinted on her audience's
memory. The message of the metaphor—"teach them to
fish"—dovetails with her call to action: Invest in our franchises.

USE ANECDOTES (BUT SPARINGLY)

Some speech counselors strongly advocate the use of
anecdotes in speeches. My experience has been that many
CEOs are uncomfortable with anecdotes. Using them well
requires a story-telling ability that many executives lack.
Moreover, some CEOs regard anecdotes as hopelessly
"corny."

Most speakers are more comfortable with "personal stories." That approach is certainly preferable to culling marginally appropriate anecdotes from a book.

There are some anecdotes, however, that seem to work in just about any circumstance. For instance, take the case when an organization or individual is the recipient of some dubious distinctions—finishing at the bottom in a sales contest, or being the leading scorer for a team that loses every game.

In that case, you might use Abraham Lincoln's story about the man who was tarred and feathered and run out of town on a rail. Someone asked the man what the experience was like. He said, "If it wasn't for the *honor* of the thing, I'd rather have walked."

Another anecdote that's useful in a variety of circumstances is the one about the elderly woman approached by a pollster on election day. He asked her, "Ma'am, which candidate did you vote for?"

She replied, "Vote? I *never* vote. It only *encourages* them."

One CEO used that story in a "Be sure and vote message." He told his audience not to emulate the old lady's example.

One warning about anecdotes. If they're longer than 30 to 35 words, don't use them. There's nothing more boring than a speaker droning on with some anecdote while members of the audience look at their watches.

USE QUOTES (BUT KEEP THEM BRIEF)

Quotations in presentations are like anecdotes—best used in moderation. Nothing paralyzes a presentation quite like a speaker reading a long quote—defined as one of 25 words or more. A well-chosen, brief quote, however, can serve as a hook to get the audience's attention.

For example, if your remarks deal with the lessons learned from a difficult experience, you could emulate the

CEO who used this quote to open his remarks: "Somebody once said, 'Life is a terrible teacher. It gives you the test before it teaches you the lesson.' "

Rohm and Haas's Larry Wilson quoted U.S. Senator (and former All-American basketball player) Bill Bradley. The point was about the need to practice skills to keep them sharp. Bradley had talked about how, as a basketball player, he had disliked practice. But he forced himself to practice assiduously. Why? "Because when you're not practicing, someone, somewhere is. And if you don't practice, when you meet that person in competition, he will win."

USE STRIKING IMAGES

Another way of making statements memorable is to use striking images. This involves using words that appeal not only to our minds, but to our senses of smell, hearing, taste, sight, or feel.

For example, John Morgan, vice president of C & P Telephone, spoke to U.S. Treasury employees about the "cultural change" that had taken place at regional telephone companies. Previous to the break-up of AT&T, the telephone business had been monolithic and monopolistic. AT&T's culture had been bureaucratic and conservative; it was unaccustomed either to competition or to a consumer focus.

Taking the Plunge

Morgan asked his audience: "How has competition changed our culture?" He answered, "About the same way a September plunge in the North Atlantic would affect a Jamaican. Shocking at first, but not really so bad after you get used to it."

What if Morgan had relied on abstractions to communicate his point? He probably would have retained the "shocking at first . . ." part of his statement. He would have left out some key images: the Jamaican and the September plunge in the North Atlantic. But those are the most memorable parts in the paragraph. In fact, everyone who's ever jumped into cold water (or stepped into a cold shower) will respond to those images.

In his speech to the Treasury Department, Morgan reinforced his picture of cultural transformation with another image. He said his company "is a virtual laboratory of cultural change. It's like a concert pianist being plunked down in the backfield of the Washington Redskins."

As Morgan demonstrates, unexpected images can be humorous as well as memorable. That's also true of an unexpected image used by Robert Buckley of Allegheny International. In a speech discussing how large, bureaucratic companies tend to stifle the innovative, entrepreneurial spirit, Buckley said: "In a centralized company, entrepreneurs are rare as polar bears in Pittsburgh."

The unexpected polar bears/Pittsburgh image brings together two disparate elements. It's the same technique advertisers use when they show a sports star in an unexpected setting—for example, basketball player Charles Barkley in fox-hunting regalia.

Most presenters can come up rather easily with unusual images. Just let your mind connect things we don't usually associate: Bengal tigers in Buffalo . . . football player William "The Refrigerator" Perry dancing the lead in "Swan Lake" . . . Robin Leach ("Lifestyles of the Rich and Famous") bedding down in a homeless shelter . . . your firm's head accountant taking up sky diving or mud wrestling . . . and so on.

REPEAT, REPEAT, REPEAT

Another way to make your lines memorable is to rely on repetition of words or sounds. Advertising relies on this technique, sometimes *ad nauseam*. What the advertisers know is that repeated words and sounds tend to impress themselves on the brain.

Jim Lynn, former CEO at Aetna used this approach. In a speech to insurance agents, I suggested to Lynn a line that read: "The most important thing the company can offer agents is: service." Lynn added the word "service" twice, so the sentence read: "The three most important things the company can offer its agents are service . . . service . . . service." The repetition calls attention to itself, and it calls attention to the point the speaker is making.

You can make up your own versions of the "service" sentence. For example, a football coach talking about the "six most important things in football. They are blocking and tackling . . . blocking and tackling . . . and blocking and tackling." Or a real estate salesperson talking about changing attitudes: "The three most important things in real estate used to be: location . . . location . . . location. Now the three most important things are: price . . . price . . . and then location."

PARALLELISM

Robert Buckley liked to blend repetition of certain phrases with *parallelism*, the repetition of grammatical and syntactical units. In one speech, he talked about how inflationary periods tended to mask poor marketing and manufacturing practices.

Buckley said, "During inflationary times raising prices becomes a way of life. Is your productivity poor? *Raise prices.* Is your marketing lackluster? *Raise prices.* Is your product mix unattractive to consumers? *Raise prices.* Is your investment philosophy unsound? *Raise prices.*"

Buckley's approach combines parallelism (asking questions) and repetition ("Raise prices"). This technique has an almost hypnotic effect on an audience. Listeners perk their ears, waiting to hear the patterns of language repeat themselves.

Consider the use of parallelism by an Aetna executive. Comparing our progress through life with climbing a mountain, he says, "The higher you go—in business or life—the harder it gets. The pack gets heavier. The trail gets steeper. The legs get wearier."

ALLITERATION

In his statement on how companies raise prices during inflationary periods, Robert Buckley concluded by using alliteration. He asked, "And who gets hurt? First, the consumer . . . then, the companies who price themselves out of the market . . . and, finally, the country."

Alliteration also lends itself well to blunt eloquence. It reinforces the rapid-fire, "boiled down" approach so favored by executives. We see this in a speech by American Electric Company president Clyde Moore. Seeking to inspire and challenge employees, Moore said, "In business, success doesn't come easy. It takes *d*rive. It takes *d*etermination. It takes *d*edication."

John Morgan of C & P used alliteration effectively to describe his company's move toward a more participative, democratic structure. He said the company's goals were now "*r*estraint rather than *r*ule-by-directive . . . *d*elegation rather than '*d*o-it-my-way.'"

Rohm and Haas's Larry Wilson takes a similar approach in a speech about the importance in manufacturing of doing it right the first time. Why is this important, Wilson asks? "Because," he adds, "*r*ejects cost money. *R*eturns cost money. *R*eworks cost money."

Wilson's predecessor at Rohm & Haas, Vince Gregory, also used alliteration in a speech to financial analysts. Summing up his experience as CEO, Gregory said: "*P*redictions are easy. *P*erformance is hard."

The alliteration by Buckley, Wilson, Morgan, and Gregory works. It does so because the rhetorical device reinforces their meaning. *When sound and sense reinforce each other, alliteration can be a powerful asset in presentations.*

ASSONANCE

In fact, some speakers go beyond alliteration to the repetition of vowel sounds. One insurance executive did this in a discussion of his company's decision to stop marketing certain products in some states. Those were states, he indicated, where regulators would not allow the company to earn an adequate return. He said, "Where it doesn't pay, we won't play."

This statement works because it describes accurately the company's marketing approach. The fact that the comment repeats the "p" and the "ay" sounds blends alliteration and assonance.

In most cases, the use of assonance has a humorous implication. We see this in a remark by former Allegheny International vice chairman Clayton Sweeney about the pitfalls of intellectual arrogance. He said, "I guess the moral of my story is that nobody likes a know-it-all."

ORAL PRESENTATIONS: "SAY IT AGAIN, SAM"

The rhetorical devices discussed in this chapter are relatively easy to learn and use. They are ways of gaining the audience's attention, of making sure they "get the message."

We can't assume our audience understands our point—let alone agrees with it—if we use flat, uncompelling language. It's up to the presenter to craft the message in such a way that it can't be misunderstood, or ignored. Devices like personal stories and parallelism, anecdotes and alliteration, metaphor and the masterful use of images can make our messages powerful ones.

Points to Remember:

- Heighten audience interest by using effective organization and dramatic effects.
- Keep a high level of intensity throughout your remarks.

- Deliver your key points with special emphasis.
- Construct your sentences so that they end with key words and phrases.
- Use personal stories, metaphors, striking images, and short, appropriate quotes.
- Repeat phrases, words, and sounds that help make your presentations memorable.

6

THE CALL TO ACTION: START WITH YOUR CONCLUSION

As much as audiences want to hear your information, they're more interested in your beliefs—your convictions, what Martin Luther King called "the content of your character." They want to know what you believe and what course of action you recommend.

STAND UP FOR WHAT YOU BELIEVE IN

Remember Dr. King's speeches? They were emotional, filled with moral fervor and a commitment to justice. They had another characteristic: They always asked the audience to take action: to contribute money to the cause; to join civil rights groups; or to lobby elected officials. On many occasions, King spoke in churches and asked his listeners to get out of their comfortable pews and march, which sometimes involved committing civil disobedience.

ACCOUNTANTS OF THE WORLD UNITE?

In our calls to action, most of us will not go as far as Martin Luther King. For example, suppose you're speaking to a small group of accountants about the shortcomings of a new accounting standard. You're probably not going to ask them to chain themselves to the entrance of the building housing the Financial Accounting Standards Board. You should, however, ask them to take concrete actions reflecting their opposition to the standard. These actions could include writing letters to the FASB or asking colleagues to support efforts to change the standard.

WHY HAVE YOU CALLED US HERE TODAY?

Essentially, your audience wants to know why they're listening to you. They don't really want you to "fill them in," give information; they want you to fill them up, with inspiration. They want to know what you think about your subject. Beyond that, they want to know *what actions you recommend that they take.*

IF YOU BUILD A CASE FOR IT, THEY WILL COME AROUND

Don't settle for listeners who sit there passively, perhaps nodding their heads, before they nod off. The audience needs to do something, to act, to help overcome the problem(s) you've identified or to seize the opportunities you've outlined.

Managing Your Boss by Communicating Well

For example, suppose you've asked for a meeting with your boss. You've worked hard, and you want "increased responsibilities" (a business euphemism meaning "more money and status"). Also, you've determined that if you don't make the case for these things, you won't get them.

When the meeting takes place, you want certain things to happen. A satisfying conclusion would be for the boss to promise to "put in for" the promotion and the raise. For that to take place, two things are necessary: First, you need to outline the facts that justify elevating you in status and salary; second, you need to make a clear request that the boss take the action you want—giving you a promotion and a raise.

The Last Shall Be First

At the meeting, you will want to preface your request for the raise and promotion with an outline of your accomplishments. When you make the request, it should come as no surprise to the boss. That's because you will have designed your presentation to support your conclusion: that you merit advancement.

What if you don't ask specifically for what you want? What if you just present *information* about your job performance—how hard you work, how creatively you've dealt with problems, how much you've accomplished for the organization?

When a Simple "Thank You" Is Somehow Not Enough . . .

If you just give information about yourself, your boss will listen respectfully, perhaps nod in agreement, and occasionally look at her watch. Then, she'll praise you for your good work, tell you to keep it up, and eventually usher you out of her office—perhaps patting you on the back. You will not have mentioned the raise and promotion—and neither will she. (Later, alone in her office, she'll probably wonder why you wasted her time.)

The "Information Fallacy"

Some people are a little uncomfortable with making presentations that call an audience to action. Asking the audience to act is risky. We think, "What if they're hesitant to make a commitment? What if they resent the request to do so?"

Portrait of a Fence-Sitter

Some people hedge their bets on the call to action. A communications manager at Boise Cascade exemplified this tendency to sit on the fence. He said that the company's CEO wants audiences to "walk away having been persuaded to take a course of action—or having been informed."

IF KNOWLEDGE IS POWER, INFORMATION CAN BE POWERLESSNESS

Knowledge *is* power, but only when it's used to affect the world around us.

Think about all the "informational meetings" you've attended. Sometimes they're justified as "bringing us up-to-date" on something or other. What such meetings usually provide is yesterday's news, after-the-fact information. We generally can no more influence the information we get than we can redirect the course of history. It's like receiving one of those little yellow message slips, with a check mark next to "No action required."

PRESENTATIONS: A POOR MEDIUM FOR INFORMATION

Presentations generally are a poor medium for presenting *detailed* information. The spoken word flows so rapidly that audiences can't assimilate details. In terms of its sensitivity, *the human ear is a blunt instrument; it's very poor at picking up details and other forms of specific information.*

And They Thought All They Had to Do Was Listen . . .

The better the presentation, the more demands it makes on the audience. Every presentation should outline a problem—and provide a solution. In appealing for your audience to act, you are asking it to put its imprint on the world around us.

For example, if you feel your job doesn't provide enough compensation or status, you ask the boss to solve the problem: to give you a raise and a promotion. If the local blood bank is running out of plasma, the solution is for you and your audience to roll up your sleeves. If you believe your elected representatives aren't acting in their constituents' best interests, you—and the audience—have a problem. The solution is to vote the rascals out of office and replace them with a new set of rascals.

BUT WHAT DOES AN ANALYST REALLY WANT?

Early in my career as a speech consultant, I learned to distrust the notion that "audiences want information." This revelation occurred when I was asked to help with a presentation to financial analysts. They are investment specialists who study companies carefully in order to make recommendations on purchasing, retaining, or selling certain stocks.

Over the years, I had heard repeatedly that financial analysts are as narrow as dollhouse doorways. Supposedly, they're interested only in financial facts about companies. Reputedly, they're extensions of their calculators and computers, unmoved by emotion, untouched by normal human concerns. "Just give them the numbers; that's all they want."

But Why Give Them What They Already Have?

I learned that the conventional wisdom about financial analysts was wrong. Bill Douce of Phillips Petroleum had great respect for the knowledge of oil-industry analysts. He knew they spoke regularly to investment relations specialists and other company executives. They also had access to great quantities of published information about the company. Speaking only half in jest, Douce told me, "Whenever I want to know what's really going on at Phillips . . . I ask the analysts."

Maloney's Conundrum

So I was left with a conundrum, a riddle: Everyone was telling me the analysts wanted only "information," numbers. *But they already had the numbers.* So why, in our presentations, should we give them the same numbers, tell them what they already knew?

The Analysts Want to Know Who the Speaker Is

Two people helped me solve my riddle. One was Douce. He said the analysts were interested in questions of *character*. They wanted to know what he and other Phillips top managers were like. Were they strong managers? Were they individuals who would try hard to keep their promises to investors? In his remarks to analysts, Douce emphasized his personal traits: his toughness, his optimism, his reasoning underlying investment decisions.

Another person helped me understand what the analysts really wanted. He was Frank Trimble, a speech coach for top executives. In his earlier career, he had been an investment counselor and a stock analyst. Frank confirmed my view that stock analysts were not really interested in hearing a recitation of facts and statistics they already had.

Trimble agreed with Douce's view that analysts wanted to assess the character of top management. He added, "They want to know why they should recommend their clients buy or hold a company's stock. They want management to tell them what action to take."

In other words, he was saying, the analysts wanted a call to action. They wanted presentations that helped them decide which stocks to recommend. They wanted CEO presenters to take a stand.

Modesty Is Not Part of the CEO's Job Description

Look at this way: How did the CEOs get their current jobs? By sitting around waiting to be noticed? By putting their trust in the good judgment of their superiors? The CEOs got what they wanted by making sure they were noticed. They got what they wanted *by asking for it or, when necessary, by seizing it.* So they're generally comfortable with action-oriented presentations.

What If You Ask . . . and They Say "No"?

The New Testament tells us: "Ask, and you shall receive." As many presenters know, sometimes you ask—and you receive a blank stare. Other times, you ask and the audience appears receptive. "Great speech, J.B. I'll be sure to write my congressman tomorrow." Then, the audience goes home, forgets about what you said, and does nothing. Remember, even when Billy Graham asks his audience to "make a decision" and come forward, fewer than 5 percent of the people do. In other words, a "response rate" of 5 percent isn't bad, but good speakers may do much better.

The Answer: Share Your Emotion

Strictly speaking, it's not the call to action that gets an audience to act. Neither is it the logic that supports your call to action. What gets the audience to act is your emotion, specifically, the feelings you convey about the need for the action. If your emotion is contagious, it will move the audience to follow your lead.

As a speech consultant, I've recommended on many occasions that CEOs make emotional speeches. One time, for example, David Roderick of USX (then U.S. Steel) spoke to the American Mining Congress. He gave a very patriotic speech, one asserting that mining and manufacturing had built this country. He told the miners to remind their congressional representatives of that fact. He said that the future of America was linked to the continued success of basic industries.

Later I received a call from a company PR representative (Tom Ward) who had attended the speech. I asked if the audience had liked it.

"Liked it?" Tom said. "They *loved* it. When Dave got to his conclusion, they stood and started cheering before he even stopped speaking. Some of them stood on their chairs and waved their arms and hollered."

So much for the theory that business people are calculating souls devoid of emotion. The best CEO-communicators know that while reason and facts may interest people, emotion moves them. They realize that the depth of their own emotional commitment to a plan of action determines the audience's ultimate reaction.

GE'S JACK WELCH: ONE OF THE BEST . . . AND FULL OF PASSIONATE INTENSITY

One speaker who delivers his remarks with great passion is GE's CEO Jack Welch. He's known for his commitment to communicating with employees. His favorite subject is GE's corporate bureaucracy. As one journalist puts it in *Fortune* magazine, "[Welch] regards bureaucracy as evil because it destroys productivity by distracting attention from useful work."

Welch's convictions about the evils of bureaucracy energize his comments about corporate rules and hierarchies. He chooses words carefully for their effect on his audience. For example, he describes "the cramping artifacts that pile up in the dusty attics of century-old companies: reports, meetings, rituals, approvals, and the forests of paper that seem necessary . . . until they're removed."

Thus, if we remember only 1 percent of Welch's comments on bureaucracy, we remember that: (1) he doesn't like it; (2) he believes it stifles creativity and productivity; (3) that, as the Roman Senator Cato said of Carthage, "it must be destroyed."

Of course, Welch knows that the audience shares his animosity for bureaucracy. After all, he's the chairman, and the bureaucracy has less capacity to frustrate him than it does the middle-managers who make up his audience. Welch thus becomes the champion of those he addresses, amplifying their voices and providing leadership.

The theme of the individual fighting the monolithic organization has an almost mythic significance not only for Welch, but for many CEOs.

LOOKING FOR AN HONEST ENTREPRENEUR

For example, Allegheny International's Bob Buckley spoke a few years ago to a mixed audience of successful entrepreneurs and employees of large companies. Like Welch, Buckley (a GE "alumnus") discussed the deadening hand of corporate bureaucracy. He saluted the entrepreneurs in the audience, and he challenged large corporations to learn from them.

In speaking of large companies, he noted that their founders had been creative risk-takers, entrepreneurs. But as the companies grew, they tended to be taken over by "conservers of the status quo."

He cautioned that entrepreneurs could survive in large, modern corporations "only if those companies remember that size and security are not ends unto themselves, only if they take heed not to let their sheer size crush entrepreneurs."

He then asked: "Where will we find tomorrow's entrepreneurs?" His answer: "We will find them by looking into the mirror. By accepting the need for risk. By realizing that we must accommodate ourselves to the entrepreneur—and not vice versa."

"Cast a Light So Bright . . ."

Buckley concluded with his call to action, telling them not to accept rule-by-bureaucracy: "Go back to your businesses," he told them. "Go back and preach—cajole—fight—in support of entrepreneurship. Go back and generate a light so bright and enduring that it will cast away the darkness."

FOLLOWING ONE CHALLENGE WITH ANOTHER— THE EXAMPLE OF GULF'S JAMES E. LEE

Another example of a "go back and spread the word" charge was made by former Gulf CEO James E. Lee. He was addressing a company task force charged with finding ways to reduce Gulf's costs. He was reiterating a challenge made earlier when, as he reminded them, "I challenged you to help make Gulf a leaner, more efficient company. I think you've met that challenge . . . and met it admirably."

He added, "I'm going to challenge all of you once again—to go back to your jobs and spread the word: that Gulf is on the move . . . that we're committed to becoming more competitive . . . to increasing profits . . . and to building on each of our successes."

Unlike Buckley, however, Lee did not leave the audience with a general challenge. (What, after all, does it mean to "go back and spread the word"?)

Lee concluded in this way: "At the table near the door, there's an envelope for each of you. It contains a pen and pencil set . . . showing our appreciation for the job you've done. But I'd also like you to look at this gift as a symbol . . . of the chapters in Gulf's history that remain to be written . . . of the work that remains to be done."

"PUT IT IN WRITING"

In his address to Aetna employees involved with auto, homeowners, and life insurance, senior vice president John Martin took a novel approach in his call for action. Kicking off the meeting, he discussed the business unit's poor record of profitability. He said improvements would come only through the intensified efforts of individual employees.

He drew their attention to the notepaper that had been left on the chairs. He asked each person to write down two steps he or she would promise to take to help the business during the next year. They could deal with any steps the individual felt would improve sales, service, or profitability.

Most of those in the audience assumed Martin would ask them to hand in the cards at the close of the meeting. In his closing remarks, however, he specifically asked them not to turn in the cards. Instead, he said, "Put them on your bulletin boards where you can see them every day. They'll be a reminder of the pledge you've made. They'll also be a reminder that the fate of the business is in your hands, the hands of each and every one of you."

The point is, Don't be afraid to ask an audience for what you want. Larry Cohen, a Connecticut speechwriter, once said that every speech by a political candidate should end with the following words: "Vote for me."

Similarly, every salesperson's pitch should end with the words, "Would you like to pay by check, cash, or credit card?" If you're a doctor or a dentist, your last words should not be: "Have a happy day." They should be: "Can I schedule your next appointment two weeks from today?"

WHICH WAY TO THE BLOODMOBILE?

Finally, in the call to action, the more specific the act requested, the better. Speech guru Dr. Jerry Tarver outlines an order of specificity, using the example of a speech requesting the audience to give blood.

The speaker might close with a general request: "Please give blood the next time the Red Cross is in town." Or the speaker might get more specific, saying, "Please sign the appointment sheet in the back of the room. It will give you a time and place to give blood." Most specific of all: "When you leave this room, please walk across the hall, where the

Red Cross is waiting for you to give blood." The more tangible and timely the action, the more responsive the audience will be to your call.

In other words, make the audience an offer it can't refuse, suffuse your request with emotion, and then "close the sale."

Points to Remember:

- Build your presentation around the closer, the call to action.
- Don't just tell the audience things; tell them to do something to influence the situation you describe.
- Use emotion to elicit a positive response from the audience.
- Make sure the action you request is one the audience can do quickly and effectively.

7

TARGETING REMARKS TO
AN AUDIENCE:
THE EXAMPLE OF
WILLIAM F. MARTIN

ACTUALLY, IT HELPS IF THE HORSE WAS THIRSTY TO BEGIN WITH

As the previous chapter indicated, the best way to organize a speech is to start not at the beginning, but at the end: with the closer, or "call to action." When you know what you want your audience to do, organize your remarks so they'll want to do it. That is, determine that the horse is thirsty and then lead it to water so that it will drink—and not run away.

. . . BUT FIRST, FIND OUT WHAT THE HORSE HAD FOR BREAKFAST

In developing a presentation, everything you say should take into account your audience: its knowledge, beliefs, and attitudes. Sometimes people ask me for a checklist of things they should know about the audience. I always tell them this: With important audiences, you can't know too much about them. You should know what they had for breakfast.

With such knowledge in hand, you can choose specific ideas, information, and illustrations to use with a particular audience. You choose the points that will be most effective with a particular audience, material that will encourage listeners to respond to your call to action. Those points will make up the body of your speech.

PRESENTATIONS: EXPRESSIONS OF *JUSTIFIED* EMOTION

For the most part, it's not especially important how you order the supporting points in your remarks. A presentation should develop systematically, but it's not an exercise in logic. It's more an expression of *justified* emotion. It's a sustained effort to break down any resistance the audience might have in response to your call for action.

To illustrate this point, I've reprinted in this chapter a speech by William F. Martin, Phillips Petroleum's CEO during the 1970s.

WHAT WAS AN OKLAHOMA OILMAN DOING IN MOSCOW?

Martin delivered the speech to the U.S.–U.S.S.R. Trade Council at a meeting in Moscow in early December 1978. The Trade Council was a joint U.S.–Soviet group designed to strengthen trade (nearly nonexistent then) between the two countries.

The Russians' Problem . . . And Martin's Solution

Martin's remarks were to deal with joint U.S.–Soviet oil development in the U.S.S.R., a country that was the world's largest producer of petroleum. The Russians used their high levels of production as a lever to keep their oil-hungry satellites in line. They also used it to earn valuable "foreign exchange," the western currency they needed to buy foreign goods and equipment.

But the Russians had a problem. As in the United States, oil was becoming harder to find and produce. In fact, CIA reports were indicating that Soviet oil production was about to start going down, as it had done earlier in the decade in the United States. To reverse the decline, the Soviets were going to have to drill offshore and in other environmentally hostile areas. But they lacked the technology and the expertise to do this successfully.

U.S. oil companies had what the Russians needed: technology and expertise. Phillips had discovered the first billion-barrel oil field in the North Sea. In 1978 it was producing large quantities of oil and natural gas from a field ("Ekofisk") 200 miles off the Norwegian coast, in nearly 200 feet of water.

What did the Russians have that Phillips wanted? Oil. Like many largely domestic companies, Phillips was facing declining supplies in its main area of exploration, the United States. During the 1970s supplies from other oil-producing areas, particularly the Middle East, had become increasingly uncertain. The North Sea was providing a steady flow of oil for Phillips, but what about the future?

Martin's speech reflected the conventional wisdom of the time, that worldwide reserves of oil were declining. In addition, the Middle East—where the largest oil deposits were—had become an increasingly uncertain source of supply. In 1973 the Arab oil producers had embargoed oil supplies to the West. In late 1976 and early 1977 the eastern half of the United States had experienced an especially cold winter, and there had been a severe shortage of natural gas.

The Soviets needed technology and expertise, which the United States had; and the United States needed oil, which the Soviets had, but which they were having increasing trouble finding and producing.

Let's Make a Deal

It sounded like the proverbial marriage made in heaven. There were all the elements for a deal: trading technology and expertise for oil.

But it wasn't that easy. The United States distrusted the Soviets—and so did Martin; they were afraid, in essence, that the Soviets would try to "steal" the technology and expertise. The Soviets were deeply distrustful of the capitalist oil people. They thought they would try to get Soviet oil at bargain basement prices.

For the Answer to the Riddle of the Universe, See the Following

In developing his remarks, Martin's challenge was a tough one. The question he faced was one that haunts many speakers and leaders: *How do you get people to do something they don't want to do?* As discussed in the previous chapter, the answer is, you convince them that it's in their best interest to do so. Easier said than done, but doable.

Hard-Eyed Men in Ill-Fitting Suits

Remember, this was not an era in which a Mikhail Gorbachev disbanded the Communist Party, in which a Boris Yeltsin faced down hard-line autocrats. Instead Martin made his remarks during the Cold War, a time when relations between the United States and the U.S.S.R. were chillier than a Moscow winter. The Soviet leaders were two uncongenial survivors of the Stalin era, Leonid Brezhnev and Alexei Kosygin. Both of them would be in the audience for Martin's talk.

Talk About an Eclectic Audience!

Overall, the audience would be the most important—and the most divided—group Martin would ever address. On the one side there would be the Soviet leadership, ministers, and Communist functionaries. On the other side would be chief executive officers of large U.S. corporations. The situation facing Martin was analogous to a speaker addressing a mixed audience of Christian evangelicals and militant atheists.

A Man Without Illusions

Martin had no illusions. For a time, he questioned whether it made sense for him to go to Moscow. After all, one speech was not going to convince the Russians to trade oil for technology. No matter how eloquent his remarks would be, he was not going to overcome a generation of mistrust.

But Martin did believe in the power of common sense and reason. He believed that someday the Soviets would come to their senses. They would realize that they shared mutual interests with the United States, and with U.S. oil companies.

"Better to Light One Candle than to Curse the Darkness"

In essence, he decided not to curse the darkness, but rather to go to Moscow and try to light a candle.

As his speech consultant, I was charged with finding out everything I could about the audience. Martin wanted to know everything about his audience: their background, knowledge, and prejudices. He wanted to know exactly where the Soviet's oil deposits were and what kind of equipment they had to extract it. His curiosity about the people he would address and their country knew no bounds.

The speech Martin delivered in Moscow follows. In reading it, you might pay particular attention to the way Martin links the interests of the Soviet Union and those of the United States. The language of the speech suggests a multitude of similarities in history and values between the two countries. This "identification of interests" is a crucial part of Martin's strategy in the speech.

ENERGY DEVELOPMENT:
A CASE OF MUTUAL INTEREST

William F. Martin
Chairman and Chief Executive Officer
Phillips Petroleum Company
To: The U.S–U.S.S.R. Trade Council
Moscow, The Soviet Union
December 4, 1978

Good afternoon.

In the past few years, all nations have become increasingly aware of the vital importance of energy.

Modern, industrialized societies—like the two countries represented here—have high levels of industrial activity . . . and utilize large quantities of energy. Likewise, the Third World countries recognize that, if they're going to raise their standards of living, they also need access to growing supplies of oil and natural gas.

At present, the Soviet Union and the United States are the two largest producers of oil and natural gas . . . and the two largest consumers of those fuels. Both nations—and especially the Soviet Union—have large undiscovered resources of petroleum. And both countries need to find and produce additional energy to maintain strong industrial bases . . . and to provide for the needs of their citizens.

It's said, "Those to whom much is given, much is demanded in return." I believe that the Soviet Union and the U.S.—the world's greatest producers of energy—have a responsibility to the people of the world. Most of those people do not share our resource bases, but they do share our hope for a better life.

We're all familiar with some of the more pessimistic forecasts about the world's energy future. Some observers say that, as demand for oil begins to exceed production, the industrialized countries will engage in highly competitive bidding . . . for oil. Under those conditions, the energy needs of the Third World could be shoved aside . . . with crippling economic effects. The industrialized world can avoid this bleak scenario. We can do so if we lead the world by example . . . and accept certain important responsibilities.

One responsibility we share is to conserve. We know that oil and natural gas are finite resources. However, they must continue to be the mainstays of our energy supply . . . into the twenty-first century. We are learning . . . sometimes with difficulty . . . how to produce more goods with less energy. In the foreseeable future, conservation will become a way of life.

Along with conservation, we should vigorously seek out the petroleum resources that are yet to be discovered. An important responsibility of the industrialized nations will be to develop the full potential of their petroleum resources. That will buy the time needed to develop new energy sources for the twenty-first century.

Oil and gas are the bridges that lead to an energy future whose outlines are not yet clear. That energy future may include such promising sources as solar energy . . . nuclear fusion . . . and other possibilities. And this points up a third important responsibility: our need to work together on long-range projects to help solve mankind's energy problems.

Right now, in Moscow, Soviet and American scientists are working together . . . at your Institute for High Temperatures. Through their joint efforts, they're searching for a means of producing inexpensive electric power . . . through a process called magneto-hydrodynamics.

This week, in the United States, other scientists from our two countries are meeting to advance their knowledge about this new source of energy. These efforts and similar ventures can help provide secure supplies of energy for the next century.

But the purpose of our meeting here is not to look far into the future. It's to consider the best possible means of meeting our needs for the near term. Foremost among these needs is to increase supplies of conventional energy, of oil and natural gas. How we meet this challenge can be one of the keys to future relationships between our two countries.

Right now, we share a common problem: one of keeping petroleum production high . . . in the face of mounting demand.

In the early years of this century, supplying petroleum was not a problem for either of our countries. Today, the search for petroleum is much more difficult and costly. Like you, we have drilled wells deeper . . . and in remote areas under hostile conditions. And we have to deal with the probable eventuality encountered in any oil reservoir: the steady decline of production.

Thus, there's a need to use better technology, not only to find more oil, but also to develop the full potential of fields already in production.

In the face of related challenges, both our countries are developing new techniques . . . and learning new skills. And the skills we're learning . . . complement one another.

For example, the expertise of the U.S.S.R. in the long-distance transmission of natural gas—particularly from tundra areas—could have application in North America. As you may know, the United States and Canada are preparing to develop substantial gas reserves in the far north, and pipeline transportation of this gas poses major problems.

On the other hand, the technology developed by U.S. petroleum companies can be combined with Soviet expertise to accelerate deep-water and frontier exploration here in your country. There also are opportunities for U.S. and Soviet oil specialists to work together on enhanced recovery techniques (that is, to extract more oil from partially depleted fields).

In fact, much of the same technology used by American companies to develop the offshore areas of Western Europe could be used to facilitate exploration and production from areas such as the Caspian Sea.

My own company has learned a great deal in developing the Ekofisk area fields in the North Sea. Despite many obstacles, including high seas and bad weather, we were able to bring the first field into production in only 18 months.

Experts tell us that while the Caspian Sea offers the possibility for the immediate application of current technology, the Barents Sea, which I'm informed has a geological setting similar to the North Sea, holds promising long-range possibilities.

Through our pioneering efforts at Phillips, we have developed new technology for exploration and production in hostile environments. New technology also has important applications for oil fields now in production. For example, chemical injection is now being used successfully in the United States. Through one new method, our company has quadrupled production in a pilot project.

These opportunities to increase oil and gas supplies can provide a foundation for our two countries to build understanding and to advance trade. Both countries, understanding one another's viewpoints and problems, can build a framework for better trade relations . . . and for better relations overall.

It's in the best interests of the world that Soviet oil and gas production remain at high levels. That will help ease the world situation with oil supplies. It will provide the Soviet Union with secure energy supplies . . . and with foreign currency . . . currency that you can use in trade with others.

American oil companies have worked closely with companies and governments in countries throughout the world. And we look forward to building similar relationships with the U.S.S.R.

We believe that, by working together, our two nations can play a key role in helping solve the world's energy problems . . . for our benefit and the benefit of our children.

Like many of you in this room, I'm a grandfather. I have three granddaughters. Being a grandfather, I was especially moved by the story of Tanya Savicheva . . . which I learned of a few days before coming here. As the Soviets here know, Tanya's entire family perished during the terrible siege of Leningrad. A haunting line in her diary has these words: "All are dead . . . only Tanya is left."

Those words make us think of our own children and grandchildren . . . and the hopes we have for their futures.

World War II was a sad time for mankind . . . and especially for the people of the Soviet Union. But it was also a time of great achievements for our peoples. We overcame our difficulties and disagreements in the face of a common threat. And, working together, we rid the world of a great menace.

Today, we face a menace that is less visible . . . but no less threatening to the Tanyas of today . . . to our young people: the threat of energy shortages . . . and the suffering they can cause.

We can overcome this challenge . . . as we overcame the earlier threat . . . by working together, trading together, and learning together. In this way, we can live together . . . in peace and prosperity.

The fruits of our cooperation on energy problems will not go primarily to those of us in this room. They will go to the generations that follow us. But it is our responsibility to make the first steps together . . . on the way to a better, safer, more secure future.

As a Speech, Not Exactly a "Piece of Cake"

That's the speech Martin delivered. I doubt that he ever worked harder on a presentation.

The Cold War as a "Terrible Misunderstanding"

As mentioned previously, the speech continually emphasizes the "common ground" between the Soviets and the

United States. It's a speech whose underlying theme is, we are people with deep and abiding common interests. Martin was asking implicitly, why argue and threaten one another when we have so much in common?

Of course, that's exactly the opposite of the view held in both countries during the 1970s. In Martin's remarks, however, the identity of interests seems credible. The "Cold War" becomes some sort of unfortunate misunderstanding.

When in Russia, Do as the Russians Do (Sort of)

The approach Martin took reflects the research we did into the audience and its concerns. His remarks are somewhat more formal than most American speeches. We learned that speeches given by the leaders of the U.S.S.R. were less colloquial, less conversational than those in our country.

They also tended to be significantly longer than the 15-minute special that was becoming the norm for speeches in the United States. But we determined that a short, powerful speech would be more effective than a long disquisition. So Martin's speech took about 20 minutes to deliver.

Winning Minds . . .

One thread of Martin's speech is the rational, business-like approach. He tells the Soviets that the United States can help them achieve goals in energy and economics. The United States has technology and expertise they can use to increase oil production. In so doing, the Soviets can get more of the foreign currency they need to buy foreign technology and goods.

Another rational argument he uses is the cooperation already taking place between United States and Soviet scientists on energy research. Thus, he says, the approach I'm suggesting makes sense, and it's a logical extension of what's happening already.

And Winning Hearts . . .

But the most powerful thread running through Martin's remarks is emotional. An accountant by training, Martin was not comfortable with emotion. However, he was, first and foremost, a pragmatic American businessman. He did not measure ideas by some sort of rigid ideological test. He valued "what worked." Thus, he was willing to take the approach that was necessary to advance Phillips' business purposes.

He was aware that mere reasoned argument was not going to open up the Russian oil fields to Phillips. The Soviets' aversion to doing business with the capitalist West was visceral, historical, and emotional. Thus, it had to be overcome not only by logic, but also by unleashing other, more positive emotions.

Martin's Challenge to the Audience: Prove That Your Rhetoric Isn't Empty

Therefore, early in his remarks Martin speaks about the common Soviet–U.S. obligation to help the oil-short Third World countries. Soviet rhetoric at the time was full of statements of solidarity with the underdeveloped countries. Martin is subtly using those statements as part of his argument for cooperating on oil development.

World War II as Precedent . . . and Emotional Bond

Another major point he raises is U.S.–Soviet cooperation in World War II. He knew that that conflict, in which 20 million Soviet citizens died, was a defining moment in the lives of his audience, particularly for the Soviet participants. Necessity and common sense, he is saying, dictated that we cooperate in the struggle against Hitler. Some of the same imperatives are present now in the battle against energy shortages.

"Tanya" and the Evocation of Emotion

The emotional climax of Martin's speech occurs when he refers to the sad story of Tanya Savicheva. She has a role in the Russian consciousness roughly analogous to that of Anne Frank in the West. For the Russian people, Tanya is a symbol of the horror and sadness of war, especially as it affects children.

I'd read the story of Tanya in Raymond Price's book *With Nixon.* Price wrote the address President Nixon delivered in Moscow in 1974, the first speech by an American leader broadcast nationwide on Soviet television. Nixon used the story of Tanya in his speech to the Russian people. Price notes in his book that he saw Russian workers weeping as Nixon told the story of the brave little girl of Leningrad.

(Martin wanted to make certain his speech did not strike any false notes, so when I told him about Tanya, he asked, "How would I have known about her?" I said, "I just told you." In the speech, he refers to Tanya's story which, he says, "I learned of a few days before coming here.")

And Little Children Shall Lead Them . . .

Martin and I had discovered that children had great value in Soviet society. Perhaps because the adults had so little in material terms, children represented hope for the future. Thus, for a child to die young, as Tanya did, was a special calamity. For an innocent child, an eloquent child, to die at the hands of Hitler's legions was to bring two powerful symbols together.

Tanya and the Picture on the Desk

When I brought the story of Tanya to his attention, Martin was moved. He looked at me, and then looked at a picture of his grandchildren on the desk. He then suggested we add the lines that begin, "Like many of you, I'm a grandfather."

Martin's speech uses rhetoric in an attempt to move people who, in their heart of hearts, did not want to be moved. In a sense, its argument is simple. It makes the case that cooperation is better than confrontation. At the same time, there is nothing in the speech that Martin did not believe. He believed in peace rather than war, in prosperity rather than poverty. He believed, as he often said, that "from those to whom much is given, much is demanded in return." He (and the United States) were ready to give; the speech was asking only that the Soviets also "ante up."

"Something There Is that Doesn't Love a Wall" (Berlin or Otherwise)

Martin's speech is a sustained effort in breaking down barriers. Pervading the remarks is an emphasis on mutual interest, on cooperation, on overcoming differences. In a subtle way, the remarks are designed to shame the ideologues who resist cooperation.

One Speech Does Not a Cold War Thaw

Did the Martin speech work? In one sense, no. In 1978 the Soviets did not jump at the offer of technology and expertise for oil. One speech could not overcome a half century of fear and suspicion. The Cold War went on, and the productive capacity of the Soviet oil industry continued to erode.

A Speech Ahead of Its Time

But in another sense, the spirit of the Martin speech did prevail. Thirteen years after Martin spoke, the Communist empire was in ruins. Free market thinking was in the ascendancy. The Berlin Wall had come down. The Soviet Union had collapsed. Boris Yeltsin, the Russian leader, had successfully resisted a hard-line coup. Nuclear disarmament was proceeding with incredible speed. And the former Soviet Union was welcoming assistance from Western businesses, including oil companies.

Presentations as a Process

The essence of Martin's 1978 remarks was the same one that prevailed in the Soviet Union in the early 1990s. In other words, his message was "before its time." That's something that has happened many times throughout history.

For example, in 1964 Ronald Reagan delivered his basic conservative message in support of Barry Goldwater. Some Americans found Reagan's Goldwater-era remarks compelling, but most apparently did not. Sixteen years later, Reagan was delivering essentially the same message, and it got him elected President of the United States and reelected four years later. It had taken a long time, but Reagan's message had gotten through.

Was Mikhail Listening?

In Bill Martin's case, his speech did not end the Cold War. But, just perhaps, it was one of the elements that touched a man who would have been in the audience, the rising Party bureaucrat Mikhail Gorbachev.

In any case, thirteen years after it was delivered, the Martin speech remains a model of how to address a skeptical audience. In its blend of reason and emotion, of common sense and moral vision, it continues to offer a good example of civilized discourse.

Points to Remember:

- Know your audience thoroughly.
- Develop your arguments, illustrations, and ideas based on the attitudes and beliefs of the audience.

- Emphasize the common interests you (and the interests you represent) have with the audience.
- Concentrate on doing everything necessary to make the audience heed your call to action.

8

PRACTICE MAKES (ALMOST) PERFECT

Practice is to presentations what spring training is to baseball: hard and unglamorous work, but essential to success.

"SPEECH? NEVER SAW IT BEFORE"

Most presentations are not adequately rehearsed, and they show it. I once saw the CEO of a New York-based corporation stumble through a speech at his company's annual meeting. He mispronounced two words in his opening sentence. I doubted he'd ever looked at the document before he mounted the podium. His speech was well written, but one wouldn't have known it from his presentation.

Did this tongue-tied CEO regard the meeting with his company's owners as unimportant? His company had spent a great deal of money putting the meeting together; dozens of the top executives from the company had flown to the meeting site. Hundreds of shareholders had spent their time and money to attend. They were there to hear the chairman report on "their" company and its stewardship of their money. Instead, they heard him demonstrate his lack of interest in the event.

LEARN FROM THE ATHLETES AND ACTORS

Presenters need to take a page from the practice of athletes and actors. A sprinter who specializes in the 100-yard dash might run in 20 meets a year. That adds up to about 200 to 220 seconds, or roughly 3½ minutes, "performing." That same athlete may practice 6 to 8 hours a day, 300 or more days per year. A professional golfer or tennis player might hit 300 or more practice shots a day.

And what actor would perform a role without extensive rehearsal? Without memorizing lines? Without trying out alternative ways of playing a scene? Without making one effort after another to get difficult scenes just right? Without practicing the actions and intonation that bring a character to life? In the movie *The Sunshine Boys*, the character played by Walter Matthau is certain he "doesn't want to do the show" with his retired ex-partner, played by George Burns. But, Matthau adds, they have to rehearse, because "Rehearsal is *important*."

WORDS THAT DIDN'T EXACTLY GO "DOWN THE HATCH"

Rehearsing presentations is important. You will never know how a presentation will sound until you practice it. For example, as I was writing this chapter, I heard Senator Oren Hatch make a speech in support of the nomination of Clarence Thomas for the Supreme Court. Hatch had trouble with several words. He stumbled over the word "applicant" in the phrase "applicant pool." And he read the word "embed" initially as "imbue," and then corrected himself.

Senator Charles Grassley of Iowa did Hatch one better. He referred to Judge *Thomas* as "Judge Thompson." (Later, another Senator referred twice to Thomas' accuser, Anita Hill, as "Mrs. Thomas"!) Senator Howard Metzenbaum, referring to the fact that Thomas apparently had no judicial position on abortion, said: "Judge Thomas, that's just *incredulous*." He didn't mean "incredulous," which means "unbelieving." Apparently, he meant *incredible*, which means unbelievable.

Of course, the Senators—like most of us—are busy people. They would claim that they didn't have time to practice their statements, most of them written by staff members. But did they really want to make statements that made them seem inarticulate, if not uninformed?

When Oratory Is Garbled, We Learn the True Meaning of the Saying "Silence Is Golden"

As a general rule, if you don't have time to practice a presentation, then don't accept the invitation to give it. Otherwise, you're taking the risk that you won't sound credible. Make enough blunders, and you'll make a fool of yourself.

WHEN IN PLATTSBURGH . . .

And don't forget: Practicing a presentation means reading it *aloud.* There are many words familiar to us in print that we hardly ever vocalize. That's why most speakers have trouble pronouncing words—such as *applicant* or *litigant* or *posterity* or *retrospect* or *paradigm.* A while ago, a television announcer in Vermont started a sentence about a Plattsburgh, New York, politician with the following words, "Plattsburgh independent candidate . . . " The announcer didn't even make it through the first word.

If a presenter has problems with certain words, it may signal a need to change them. For instance, insert some articles and prepositions in the "Plattsburgh" example: "John Smith is an independent running for mayor of Plattsburgh." The additions make the statement more readable; they don't confront the speaker with one unpronounceable word after another.

JUST BE HAPPY HE DIDN'T REFER
TO ZBIGNIEW BREZINSKI

Speech writer Rodger Morrow tells a story about a speech he wrote for a corporate executive. The executive liked the speech, but then he asked, "Exactly who is this guy Mace-ee-uh-vel-ee?" Morrow had referred to the seventeenth-century Italian political philosopher Niccola Machiavelli, pronounced "Mack-ee-uh-vel-ee." (It's a good thing the executive asked the question before going on stage.)

A STRANGE THING HAPPENED WHEN I OPENED
MY MOUTH

Even with fairly simple words, our minds and eyes can play tricks on each other. For example, one CEO I worked with had a terrible time with the word "country," as in "our country." Every time he read it, the word came out "company," a term that apparently came easily to his lips. The solution was easy: I had him change "country" in his scripts to "nation."

Passages that are hard to read are difficult to detect visually. Bill Douce of Phillips told me that reading aloud was the only way he could spot "tongue twisters." He was referring to words that demand more physical effort in the mouth to pronounce. These include words with "gr" sounds (grind, grimace), or "sn" sounds (snake, snarl). They also include some alliterative phrases ("The pipelines' potential plusses and minuses") that are as hard to get through as "Peter Piper picked a peck of pickled peppers."

WOULD THE CEO HAVE SAID, "YOU WHO DID THIS
TO ME ARE *FIRED?*"

One potential blunder that never made it to the rehearsal stage involved a speech for David Roderick of USX, a corporate "tough guy." An individual who reviewed

Roderick's speeches had the irritating habit of inserting irrelevancies in speech drafts. On the speech, the reviewer insisted a certain sentence needed the word "you" inserted.

Did He Say What I Thought He Said?

I looked at the sentence and saw the word after the insert was "who," as in "you who have done so much to build this industry." I raised the question: "How would it look if a steel company CEO were to blurt out 'Yoo hoo'?" Thereafter, the reviewer refrained from making inserts.

ACCENTUATING THE POSITIVE: HIGHLIGHT KEY POINTS

Rehearsals can also highlight instances where speakers are "throwing away" words and phrases that deserve emphasis. *As speakers read through final drafts of their presentations, they should do so with pen in hand.* That way, they can underline words and phrases that need emphasis.

Recharge Your Oratorical Batteries

They can also determine where their energies are waning and can note where physical and mental efforts are needed to "turn up the intensity level." As indicated previously, all speakers tend to lose speed. They begin to get tired; they react unconsciously to the audience's "declining attention curve." They start forgetting to vary the pitch and emphasis of their voices, falling into a monotone.

INTENSITY Means: "Turn It Up a Notch"

In their rehearsals, speakers can pinpoint the places in the presentation where their intensity begins to flag. When that happens, presenters should mark their speech or note text in capital letters with the word *INTENSITY*. Every time they see that marginal note during the presentation, they can give themselves a shot of mental and verbal adrenaline.

In sports, this revivified effort is called "turning it up a notch."

In Practicing, Two (or More) Heads Are Better than One

Practicing your presentations alone can be useful. You can spot words and passages that need attention. But, in fact, solo rehearsals do not really simulate the situation presenters face. The essence of a presentation is that it's made to an audience—one that responds with interest or uninterest, with quizzical or knowing looks, with polite or enthusiastic applause.

Is That What's Meant by "For Better or For Worse"?

In rehearsing their presentations, smart speakers seek out "constructive critics." In two decades of work with two dozen CEOs (all of them male), I've been amazed by how many of them rehearsed with their wives. I learned about this widespread practice when corporate spouses would come up to me and comment on their husbands' speeches—before they'd been delivered. There's nothing wrong with reading speeches to spouses. Sometimes, however, those who are sworn to "love, honor, and cherish" seek to shield us from unpleasant truths.

WHEN FLATTERY WILL GET YOU NOWHERE, TRY HONEST CRITICISM

When practicing your speech, seek out people who will assess your presentations objectively. This might be a spouse or a "significant other." More likely, it will be a friend, a co-worker, or even a member of your organization's public relations staff. If possible, get someone who's known to be an effective presenter.

With your constructive critic in tow, go through your presentation. Try to make this rehearsal as real as possible, anticipating the exact circumstances you'll encounter in the presentation. In other words, if you're going to speak from a lectern, find one and use it. If you'll have a microphone, get one for your rehearsal. If there will be a Q & A, have the constructive critic fire interrogatory "hard balls" at you.

THE TAPE IS A TOUGH CRITIC

Be sure to tape your rehearsal, on videotape if possible. John Young, Hewlett-Packard CEO, notes to a business journalist that he has had "quite a bit of formal television training." He adds, "It's quite an exacting medium. It always magnifies those little glitches in your delivery."

If you don't like what you see on the tape and what you hear from your constructive critic, go through another "take." That is, go through the presentation again—and again and again—until you get it right.

AS THE POET SAID, "IF WE HAD WORLD ENOUGH AND TIME, THIS COYNESS . . . WOULD BE NO CRIME"

Top executives who are good communicators *always* find the time to rehearse. Top executives who are poor communicators *never* have the time to rehearse.

At times, you may have to encourage other people to rehearse. This is particularly true when you're asked to write a speech "for the boss." You may write an excellent presentation, but it won't live up to its potential if the presenter doesn't practice. So it's very much in the writer's interest to make certain the client rehearses.

Most clients agree that rehearsal would be desirable. Then they add, "If I just weren't so busy." They agree, theoretically, that it would be a good idea, if they just had the time.

When Suggestions Fail, Try Trickery

When confronted with such excuses, it's up to speech writers and their allies to use trickery. For example, as a speech consultant, I've had to use various stratagems to get unwilling executives to rehearse.

In one case, an executive client of mine was experimenting with the use of a TelePrompTer. I told him it was essential that we "check" the prompter so that nothing would go wrong during the formal presentation. Executives don't like to think about "things going wrong," so he put the "Teleprompter check" on his schedule. That check involved having him read through his presentation—rehearse it, in other words.

Invariably, the executive would spot weak or questionable passages and have us make changes. When the executive delivered the now-familiar presentation, he or she invariably did it well.

TAKE ONE, TAKE TWO

At Gulf Oil, Chairman Jim Lee made numerous videotapes for employees during the attempted takeover of the company. In his case, he really was busy, trying to fend off an effort to grab the company he led. When we were ready to do the videotapes, we had him do two takes. Of course, the first take was the rehearsal, the second the actual shooting.

For speech consultants, deviousness is sometimes essential.

Companies increasingly recognize the need for rehearsal. For important meetings, Aetna's Canadian subsidiary assigns its executives a specific time to rehearse. When Aetna officers from the United States were going to address an Aetna Canada meeting, times would be set aside for them to rehearse. This technique would make the U.S. officers, who usually didn't like to rehearse, feel guilty about not doing so. In most cases, they'd show up at their allotted time.

At Gulf, it was common practice to have rehearsals complete with professional speech coaches. The coaches would videotape rehearsals of upcoming presentations. Then they'd review the videotapes with Gulf executives and offer advice on content and delivery.

Of course, most presenters can't afford—or don't have access to—professional speech coaches (whose services might cost $200 an hour, or more). But with the help of this book, coupled with the "constructively critical" assistance of a friend or associate, you can rehearse as productively as the CEOs.

IS ALL THIS WORK WORTH IT?

How much time should you put into rehearsal? That depends on the presentation's significance. If it's important to your career and/or to your organization's success, you can't rehearse enough.

Rehearsal is a way of transferring "ownership" of a scripted speech. It's a way of seeing which words and phrases are out of character and a way of making necessary changes. It's a way of making the speaker comfortable with the text. That ensures it can be delivered with skill and conviction.

HOW "AVERAGE" SPEAKERS CAN DELIVER
GREAT SPEECHES: BUSH AND DUKAKIS

A good speech can affect the course of history. For instance, look at the effect two speeches had on the presidential election of 1988. The leading candidates, Michael Dukakis and George Bush, were not inspiring orators. In fact, many commentators wondered what these men stood for. What was their vision? How did they propose to lead America in the last decade of the twentieth century?

These questions converged to give great importance to the candidates' acceptance speeches. To the surprise of many people, both candidates met the challenge.

In their book *Whose Broad Stripes and Bright Stars*, Jack Germond and Jules Witcover described Dukakis' performance this way: "The audience in the [Louisiana] Superdome cheered and applauded long and loud, and even in the network anchor booths, the hardened oracles of the television era spoke in laudatory terms of his performance." History had thrown Dukakis a high, hard fastball—and he drove it out of the park. Dukakis went into the convention with a six-point lead in the polls. He came out with a double-digit lead.

A few weeks later, George Bush delivered his acceptance speech at the Republican convention. It was a speech that introduced the country to Bush's themes of a "kinder, gentler nation" and "a thousand points of light."

Time magazine summed up Bush's performance this way: "Vice President [Bush] delivered a stirring acceptance speech that was the equal of Michael Dukakis' oratorical triumph in New Orleans. In a strong, I'm-the-guy-in-charge voice, Bush fused masterful metaphors and political put-downs with his campaign themes of family, freedom, and the future."

How did two gentlemen with reputations as indifferent orators turn the situation around? They did it by taking the time to work hand in hand with talented writers. And they did it by a continuous process of reviewing speech drafts and rehearsing their presentation.

About Dukakis' preparation, we know that he worked hard before and during the convention to make sure the speech communicated the themes he wanted to get across. When he made the speech, he knew it so well, and it reflected his views so clearly, that it dramatically improved his public standing.

We know a great deal about the preparation of George Bush's acceptance speech. His speech writer, Peggy Noonan, describes the genesis and gestation of his speech in her superb book *What I Saw at the Revolution*. Noonan, Bush, and his campaign staff approached the acceptance speech as if it were the Battle of Armageddon.

Bush and Noonan met many times about the speech. He gave her copious notes about issues he wanted covered in the speech. She probed his ideas, his values, his personal history. She encouraged Bush to put his ideas on paper, to define exactly what he saw as the differences between him and his opponent.

Bush delivered the speech well. He did so not only because he had practiced his delivery assiduously, but also because the speech had become so much a part of him, so much a part of the fiber of his being.

Practice does more than use repetition to improve delivery skills. Practice forces the presenter to look inward, to ask: Is this really what I want to say? Is this word, this phrase, this speech a reflection of who and what I am?

Practice also forces the presenter to look outward, toward the audience. It raises the questions: Is what I'm saying really what the audience wants to hear? How can I adjust my message—the words before me—in such a way as to encourage a positive response to my call for action?

THE PASTOR AND THE EMPTY PEWS

I began this chapter by discussing a CEO who obviously hadn't practiced an important presentation. This CEO's approach to practice contrasts dramatically with that of a speaker such as the Reverend Delbert Tieman, pastor of the Pinnacle Lutheran Church, near Rochester, New York.

When I lived in Rochester, my way to and from school would take me by Delbert Tieman's church. Every Friday morning I'd see him alone in church. He'd be standing at the pulpit, practicing his sermon. He'd be speaking intensely, standing before rows of empty seats. The thought occurred to me: This man cares about his sermons and his "calling" very much.

I never attended Tieman's church, but I always suspected his sermons were very good. Later, when I heard him speak on several occasions, including his delivery of the eulogy at my mother's funeral, I learned my impression was correct.

Practice didn't make him perfect. But it was an important factor in making him very good.

Points to Remember:

- Look at practice as the key to perfecting your presentations.

- Recognize that you'll never know how a presentation will sound until you rehearse it.

- Don't agree to give a presentation if you won't have time to practice it.

- Seek out constructive critics to evaluate your practice sessions.

- Learn from the example of individuals like Bush and Dukakis, who used extensive rehearsals to help them give the "speeches of their lives."

9

GRAPHICS: DON'T USE THEM UNLESS THEY'RE TRULY "GRAPHIC"

WHO WANTS TO BE MASTER OF CEREMONIES FOR A BUNCH OF SLIDES?

It's hard to imagine a *great* speech that uses graphics. Professional speech writers generally avoid them. One said that graphics "turn a speaker into an emcee for a bunch of slides."

"I HAVE A DREAM, BUT FIRST SOME VISUAL AIDS"

Graphics would not have been suitable in Bill Martin's presentation in Moscow. They wouldn't be appropriate in a presidential inaugural address or even in a State of the Union message. It's almost unimaginable to think of Martin Luther King on the steps of the Lincoln Memorial clicking up a few slides or marking up a flip chart.

Major presentations have (or should have) a seamless quality; they should reflect a process of thought and insight. In that kind of process, graphics are a distraction. Because they appeal to the eye, which is more sensitive than the ear, visual aids draw attention away from the speaker. That's apparently why President Reagan stopped using them in his televised addresses.

Don't use visual aids just because "it's traditional." Instead, start from this premise: Audio-visual aids have to earn their way into your presentation. In other words, use them when they're *necessary* to support your points.

MURPHY MUST HAVE USED GRAPHICS

Experienced speakers know that graphics can be to presentations what land mines are to battlefields. In other words, when using graphics, watch your step. Graphics can be visual illustrations of Murphy's Law. Bulbs burn out. Slide carousels stick. Flip-chart stands collapse. Vu-graphs get out of order. Letters and numbers are unreadable to anyone sitting farther back than the second row. Videotapes run in fast forward. Speakers and members of the audience trip over wires. Electricians mysteriously disappear during electrical outages.

HORROR STORY #1

Everyone who's worked with visual aids has some horror stories. For example, in the late 1970s Phillips Petroleum was invited to make a business presentation in the People's Republic of China, a major breakthrough for the company.

In part because of the language barrier, the company decided to use 35-millimeter slides to portray the company to the Chinese. Speech writers and executives ransacked Phillips' slide collections to put together illustrated presentations on oil exploration, refining and marketing, coal and uranium development, and chemicals.

A few days before the trip to China was to begin, Phillips' president Bill Douce called all the Phillips speakers together to rehearse their presentations. Speakers and a few public relations people gathered in the company's executive conference room.

Douce asked for the first presentation, which dealt with Phillips' capabilities in offshore oil exploration. The first slide appeared on the screen, followed by the second slide, which appeared not only on the screen, but also on the ceiling. Horizontal slides had been mixed with verticals.

This was the case throughout the presentation. Members of the audience—Phillips executives—alternately looked at the screen and then craned their necks to scan the ceiling.

Douce's neck also bobbed up and down. After the presentation, he said, "Well boys, I guess we've still got some work to do."

A Man Ready to Give His Life
for His Company

When the Phillips group went to China, they found the People's Republic had a unique electrical system. The electrical systems on the slide carousels would not work on the Chinese outlets. So one of the party had to don rubber gloves and hold the spliced electrical cords against the electrical apertures. He told me that during the presentations he believed he was in extreme danger of electrocution.

HORROR STORY #2: LYNDON LAROUCHE
AND THE CASE OF FLY-BY GRAPHICS

Perhaps the worst use of graphics I've seen was by Lyndon LaRouche, perennial presidential candidate, conspiracy theorist, and convicted felon. During the 1988 election campaign, LaRouche appeared on a 30-minute commercial. He was discussing his curious economic theories (which blamed most of the world's economic problems on the Queen of England and other nefarious forces in Great Britain).

LaRouche illustrated his remarks with charts. They were not the usual stationary charts used by most speakers. Instead, they were mounted on runners. As LaRouche made a point, he would press a button and a chart would pass behind him. The charts were so small that viewers could barely see them.

What's Faster than a Speeding Bullet?

As the program went forward, LaRouche started to run short of time—but not of slides. So he began to talk faster and to push his chart buttons with increasing gusto. As the camera continued to focus on LaRouche, the charts ran by him at a vertiginous pace. In fact, from the off-camera sound of things, the charts apparently began to crash into one another and pile up at the end of his runner.

I began to wonder if perhaps Queen Elizabeth II and the British Secret Service had sabotaged LaRouche's show.

Most audiovisual presentations don't fail as dramatically as Lyndon LaRouche's chaotic show. They fail through lack of drama. They fail because the audiovisual points they make are either redundant, unilluminating, or amateurish.

TITLE SLIDES: AN EXERCISE IN PRESENTATIONAL REDUNDANCY

Take what are known as "title slides." These are words and phrases flashed on a screen. In many cases they do nothing more than duplicate the words the speaker is saying. For example, the speaker is saying, "The three Baltic states are Estonia, Latvia, and Lithuania." On the screen, we see the heading, "Baltic States." Underneath are three words: Estonia. Latvia. Lithuania. Is the speaker's assumption that the audience is hearing-impaired?

WHAT IS THE SOUND OF A GRAPHIC FALLING WITH A DULL THUD?

A related form of audiovisual failure occurs when a graphic fails to make an auditory or visual point. For example, if a speaker says, "Profits have risen gradually over the past three years," how does it add to that point to use a slide that shows this gradual rise? Or, if your point is that Texas is the main oil-producing state, how does it advance your point to show a picture of a drilling rig? In other words, don't use visuals that have no purpose.

POOR-QUALITY VISUALS = POORLY RECEIVED PRESENTATIONS

A third way in which audiovisuals fail is when they're unprofessionally made. I've seen million-dollar-a-year executives use hand-drawn Vu-graphs in important presentations. Invariably, the Vu-graphs are somewhat off center, calling attention to themselves rather than to their "information." Sometimes, they're placed upside down, which offers speakers opportunities to interrupt their presentations and make awkward apologies.

Visuals: No Place for Amateurism

Poor-quality audiovisuals detract from speakers' messages and undermine their credibility. Through audiences' experience with television (and their own video cameras), they are used to professionalism. I found this out when I was in charge of Gulf Oil's video reports from the chairman. We were amazed by how many comments we received from employees about *technical aspects* of the productions. People would criticize the introductory graphics, or tell us we'd had inappropriate head shots, or indicate that certain portions of the program suffered from insufficient editing.

If your visual support is not high quality, either get professional assistance or forgo graphics.

BIG CHANGES MAKE GOOD GRAPHICS

What kind of material lends itself to good visuals? The kind that makes a striking or unusual point. For example, information that shows dramatic changes over a short period of time.

For instance, in a talk about the rapidly rising cost of health care, a speaker made the following statement: "In 1970, health-care costs in America were $75 billion. By 1985, they were $420 million." This would make a good line graph. The line would go up like a Saturn rocket, with a high point ($420 million) more than five times the height of the low point. It would present a dramatic picture of the rise in health-care costs.

Another instance where a graphic proved useful was in a talk by Jack Mulroney, president of Rohm & Haas. He was making the point that America's exports of services would not balance our large trade deficit in manufactured goods. He said, "Manufacturing exports exceed services exports by a ratio of five to one." This would lend itself to a bar graph that would illustrate the huge differential Mulroney described.

He added, "Last year, the United States had a favorable trade balance in services of $4.6 billion. But our unfavorable trade value in merchandise was $170 billion. Trying to balance trade with services is like trying to empty the Gulf of Mexico with a bucket."

Again, a bar graph would demonstrate starkly the mouse-sized favorable balance in services with the elephant-sized unfavorable merchandise balance. In fact, it might add drama to the slides by making the "services" bar a mouse and the "merchandise" bar an elephant.

SIMPLICITY: THE KEY TO VISUAL CLARITY

Graphs—line or bar—should be simple. Al Butkus, a communications manager at Bell Atlantic says line graphs should have one line, two at the most. Why? Because if they have several lines, people can't grasp their meaning. They get confused over which lines represent what. Thus, graphs should be models of simplicity and clarity—just as a presentation's spoken words are.

In support of Butkus' point: I once saw a slide with untold numbers of lines in different colors. The speaker told us apologetically that the graph illustrated "61 variables" involved with gasoline marketing. He couldn't tell one variable—let alone 61—from another, and neither could the audience. The slide was, however, very colorful.

HOT POTATOES AND WINSOME LASSES

Most executives use graphics to present statistics, but they can be used creatively to make points that are hard to convey verbally. For example, Professor Uwe Reinhardt of Princeton is a colorful and provocative speaker on America's crisis in health care. His basic point is that private health insurers are not interested in insuring those who need their services most: people in ill health.

In one of his presentations, he uses slides to reinforce this point. One slide shows a steaming potato. He asks the audience: "What is this?" Several people in the audience shout: "A hot potato."

In his next slide, Reinhardt shows a winsome child with a sad look on her face. He pauses while the image sinks in, and then he says: "This also is a hot potato. It's a sick little girl nobody wants to insure."

With this technique, Reinhardt transcends the dry statistics and rhetoric that surround the issue of health care and insurance. He uses his slides to humanize the issue—and to give it some striking emotional content. As Hollywood has known for a long time, you can't go wrong with pictures of children or dogs.

In using videotapes with presentations, the same rules apply. Try to stay away from what television people call "talking heads": videos that focus on individuals engaged in earnest conversation. Instead, use video that shows action.

For example, one video we used effectively at Aetna dealt with that company's program to combat drunk driving. We talked about the thousand-plus video cameras Aetna had donated to local police departments to aid them in making cases against drunk drivers.

We then showed a video camera in action. It was in a police car chasing a drunk driver who was trying to evade capture. The camera showed the car heading at high speed toward an intersection. Suddenly, the car being pursued swerved, but not in time to avoid broadsiding a car coming through the intersection. As the cars collided, the audience watching the video gasped.

The video conveyed what the donated cameras could do. It also showed the kind of accidents the camera's users hoped to prevent and did so better than words could convey.

The best "audiovisual aids" are those that don't require a lot of commentary. They should speak for themselves. For example, in the 1991 baseball playoff between Atlanta and Pittsburgh, the two announcers showed admirable restraint at one point. A Pittsburgh batter came to home plate, took a swing at the ball, and hit a home run.

Their Silence Was Golden

The announcers (Tim McCarver and Jack Buck) didn't say anything while the camera followed the ball as it flew over the fence and the sound system picked up the crowd's roar. As the player rounded the bases, the camera tracked his progress, and the Buck/McCarver team remained silent. Not until the home-run hitter had exchanged "high fives" with teammates and disappeared into the dugout did the announcers speak.

McCarver and Buck's restraint allowed the watcher to savor the moment (if they were Pittsburgh fans) or to rue it (if they were Atlanta fans). The two didn't belabor the obvious, trying to explain in words what was unfolding on the screen. They let the television pictures speak for themselves.

SOMETIMES *OBJECTS* ARE WORTH
A THOUSAND WORDS

When you're considering using visual aids, it some-times pays to think beyond "the usual suspects": slides, Vu-graphs, flip charts, and even video. *Some of the best visual aids are objects, things you can show the audience.*

ELECTRONIC CALCULATORS: DON'T LEAVE HOME
WITHOUT ONE FITTING SNUGLY IN YOUR WALLET

In a speech some years ago, Westinghouse CEO Robert Kirby used this technique. His speech dealt with the trend in electronics toward *miniaturization.* To illustrate his point, he held up a pocket calculator made by Sony Corporation. As he turned the calculator around so the audience could see, Kirby noted that it was hardly thicker than a credit card. He then held up his American Express card to illustrate the point.

Did this approach make his remarks on miniaturization memorable? Kirby made his talk seven years before I wrote this passage, and I remember his illustration clearly.

Another example of using an object to make a point occurred when doctors gave a newborn infant a heart trans-plant. In order to illustrate the minuscule size of the heart, one doctor held up a walnut. He indicated it was slightly larger than the transplanted organ.

Ingenious speakers can find many objects that will suit their purposes. For instance, suppose you're talking about a management initiative that encourages risk taking. With risk, of course, comes the possibility of making errors. You might illustrate your points by first holding up a pen. That could illustrate the old management, which emphasized not making mistakes. Then you could hold up a pencil—perhaps stressing that pencils have erasers—to reflect the new ap-proach.

Wisely used, visuals can enhance your presentations. The test is this: Do they tell part of your story in a way that's better than words alone? If they do, use them.

Points to Remember:

- Make audio-visual aids "earn" their way into your presentations.
- Avoid adding to the list of audio-visual "horror stories."
- Rely, whenever possible, on professionals to design and make your visual and audio aids.
- Use such aids when they make a point better than you can with words alone.
- Make sure your audio-visuals show either action or dramatic changes.

10

HUMOR: MAKING SURE THE JOKE'S NOT ON YOU

A SUBTLE DISTINCTION

For many people, the words "joke" and "humor" are synonyms. Although the word humor includes jokes, it is broader. As GE communicator William Lane puts it, "The stand-up joke is deadly, and it seldom works." But he adds that, in any presentation, humor "is the absolutely indispensable ingredient."

TOP HATS, SNOWBALLS, AND "ASPARAGITH"

Humor is the ability to see that dreariness and solemnity are not the essence of life. Humor is the snowball that moves "unerringly toward the top hat, or the foot that moves inexorably toward the banana peel. It's the television commercial where the little girl explains patiently to a lunkheaded adult that a certain green vegetable is not, as he calls it, "aspara*goose.*" It is, she exclaims, "aspara*gith.*"

WHY "WILD BILL HICKOCK" FANS
SHOULD THANK THE GAS COMPANY

Humor is "Jingles," Andy Devine, telling of the time he was so depressed early in his acting career that he decided to commit suicide by turning on the gas. After he did so, he spotted a note under his door. He picked it up and began to read. It was from the gas company. It said that since he had ignored repeated requests to pay his bill, they had turned off his gas.

NOTE TO PRESENTERS: LIGHTEN UP

Presentations generally are short on humor. In fact, they have a tendency to be excessively formal affairs. It's not a long journey from formality to stuffiness—and pomposity. The appropriate use of humor can save a presentation from excessive solemnity and self-importance. It can help establish a bond of camaraderie between speaker and audience.

START WITH A JOKE OR TWO? BOMBS AWAY!

Our old friend "Conventional Wisdom" says that presentations should begin with a funny story or two. Telling jokes effectively is a specialized skill, however—like removing gallstones or clearing away land mines. There are more "bombs" launched from America's speaking platforms every day than hit Baghdad during the Persian Gulf War.

WHEN ALL ELSE FAILS . . . JOKES
PROBABLY WILL ALSO

Why do jokes in presentations fail? Three reasons:

- The joke doesn't relate to the speech; it just lurches in inappropriately, like the town drunk at a temperance meeting;

- The speaker hasn't rehearsed the joke and tested it beforehand, so it's presented with all the timing and precision of a slip on the ice;
- The joke is an old one, and it's as appealing as yesterday morning's coffee.

Make Sure the Joke's Not on You

These cautions suggest that speakers should use jokes the way the bomb squad handles explosives: very carefully. Johnny Carson made a career out of blown laugh lines. But when noncomedians misfire, they find out the joke's on them.

Those Board Rooms Must Be a Million Laughs

Spontaneous jokesters are rare, especially among business people. One apparent exception was Ross Johnson, former CEO of RJR Nabisco, as described in the book *Barbarians at the Gate.* At a meeting of the company's Board, Johnson said he had tried a competitor company's soft cookies; he added he'd left them on his desk for a few hours, and they got stale.

One Board member, apparently assuming the Ed McMahon role, asked, "How hard were they?"

Without hesitation, Johnson fired back, "Ever try biting into a hockey puck?"

As the Johnson story illustrates, whether a joke succeeds is largely a matter of the right words and, especially, the right *timing.* If the punch line is delivered too early—or too late—the joke doesn't work.

FRANKLY, I'D RATHER BE IN ROCHESTER

Charles Osgood of CBS has a marvelous sense of timing. One joke he told related to the periodic suggestion that New York City become a state. As Osgood tells it, "The new state would be called New York." He adds, "The rest of the state would be called . . . Buffalo."

For Osgood's joke to work, there has to be a short pause after "called" and before "Buffalo." If there's no pause, there's really no effective joke. If the pause is too long, then "Buffalo" somehow gets lost, separated from the rest of the punch line.

HE SHOULD HAVE STAYED IN BED

In the wrong hands, jokes misfire as often as do fire-crackers in a rain storm. Consider the case related to me by a certain speechwriter. He had to prepare remarks for an executive who was as stiff as a week-old corpse, as funny as a toe bouncing off a bedpost.

This dour gentleman had to make a 7:30 A.M. speech to an employee audience. His prepared remarks consisted of a long recitation of well-known financial facts. The address cried out for some light opening comments.

The speech writer had an inspiration. He decided to open the speech with an old line that referred to the speaker's often-stated aversion to getting up early: "Irving Berlin once said that all *buglers* should be shot . . . preferably *before* dawn." There seemed no way the line could not work.

When the speech writer received an audio tape of the remarks as presented, he heard the speaker say the following: "Irving Berlin once said that all *burglars* should be shot. . . ." The audience erupted not into laughter, but into the seemingly eternal silence of perplexity.

HUMOR: YET ONE MORE THING THEY DIDN'T TEACH YOU AT HARVARD BUSINESS SCHOOL

Why are so few business executives blessed with good senses of humor? It may be, as one told me, that "making money is *very serious business*." Admittedly, boards of directors don't pay people a million dollars or more per annum for their talents as stand-up comedians.

A DEFINITION OF "THE GOOD,"
BUT NOT OF THE TRUE AND THE BEAUTIFUL

With jokes, there's just one rule of thumb: Don't tell them unless you're skilled at them. (In this sense, "skilled" means that your jokes get laughs from people whose jobs don't depend on your good will.)

Don't Leave Them Laughing;
Leave Them Smiling

This doesn't mean, however, that most speakers should avoid *humor*. But they should take steps to make sure they use humor effectively. Specifically, they should consider whether the humor they're considering is appropriate for the particular audience and suited to the rest of the remarks. In addition, they should practice delivering lighthearted lines with skill and style; third, they should stick generally to *light humor*.

Does It Play Well in Peoria?

One way to test appropriateness and to practice your humorous lines is to "take them on the road," as producers do with plays. That is, practice your humor on associates, friends, and family. Ask them for their candid view of whether your humor is right for a specific audience. If the humor you use is a hit in New Haven, it probably will play on Broadway.

In your efforts at humor, don't try for high-megaton laughter. Leave the side-splitters and thigh-slappers to the professional comedians. Light humor aims not for a belly laugh, but for a smile that may escalate into laughter.

FIVE WAYS TO GET AUDIENCES TO CRACK A SMILE

What kind of humor works best in presentations? There are five basic kinds:

- First, "all weather" stories;
- Second, improbable images;
- Third, self-deprecation;
- Fourth, *gentle* deprecation of others;
- Fifth, life's little absurdities.

All-weather stories: These are tales rather than jokes. They're easy for speakers to remember and thus hard to "mangle" in telling. They're also little known enough that most people in audiences haven't heard them. (In other words, they haven't been on the *Tonight* show.) Again, if you're in doubt about how widely known a story is, use the "New Haven tryout."

I gave a friend of mine an all-weather story some years ago, and he swears it was a hit at ten sales meetings that he chaired.

Brother Andrew, Would You Please Pipe Down?

The story deals with Brother Andrew, who entered a cloistered monastery in Ireland. When Andrew became a novice monk, the abbot, Brother Matthew, informed him about the order's strict vow of silence. Monks were allowed to say only two words every 10 years—and to utter them only to the abbot.

Ten years passed as Brother Andrew labored in the vineyards and endured the hardships of monastic life. Finally, he was ushered in to see Brother Matthew and to speak his two words.

Brother Andrew glared at the abbot and said, "*Bed's hard!*" Brother Matthew gave a sympathetic nod.

Another 10 years went by, and the now-bearded Brother Andrew returned for his two words. He exclaimed, "*Food stinks!*" The abbot smiled ruefully.

Another 10 years passed, and an obviously distressed and haggard Brother Andrew returned. He held himself to the two-word code, shouting: "*I QUIT!*"

As Andrew stormed out, the abbot turned to his assistant and said, "Well, it's no big loss. Ever since he came here, he's done nothing but bitch!"

The Brother Andrew story works because it reflects two facts about human nature: one, the tendency of "employees" to complain about organizations they've joined voluntarily; two, the tendency of management to interpret criticisms as indications of a thoroughly negative attitude.

Good Sports

Certain sports figures are also good sources of all-weather stories. The late Casey Stengel not only mangled the language with awesome facility, but also left us food for thought. For example, he left us the image of a baseball manager "whose limitations are . . . limitless." As one executive put it after using the Stengel story: "All of us have had those kinds of managers." He added, "Maybe some of us *are* that kind of manager!"

Yogi Also Said of a Restaurant, "Nobody Goes There Any More . . . It's Always Too Crowded"

Bill Genge, head of Ketchum Communications, used Yogi Berra to make a marketing point. Genge was describing Pennsylvania's poor record in attracting tourists prior to Ketchum's highly successful advertising campaign ("You've Got a Friend in Pennsylvania").

Genge said, "Prior to 1979, Pennsylvania's tourism situation was reminiscent of the situation of the last-place team Yogi described, where "the fans came disguised as empty seats."

Former football coach Hank Stram's star might be rising in the all-weather category, as illustrated in a statement by Gerry Mossinghoff, president of the Pharmaceutical Manufacturers Association: "After Stram's team had lost a tough game, a friend tried to console him by saying, 'Winning isn't *everything.*' Stram thought for a minute, and replied, 'Yeah, but losing isn't *anything.*' "

Is This a Case of Discrimination Against German Shepherds and Lake Michigan?

A recent—and abundant—source of all-weather humor has been the proliferation-of-lawyer stories. William O. Bailey, CEO of Municipal Bond Investors Assurance Company, is a critic of America's system of filing endless lawsuits; he believes lawyers are the culprits behind this phenomenon.

A special favorite of Bailey's is as follows: "What's brown and looks good on a lawyer?" Answer: "A Doberman." And: "What do you call 200 lawyers at the bottom of Lake Erie?" Answer: "A start."

(If there are lawyers in the audience when you tell such stories, expect two things: first, that they'll chuckle, to show they're good sports; second, that they will make a mental note that somehow, somewhere they will get you.)

All Good Things Come to an End . . .

One caution about all-weather stories: Because they're good stories and usable in a variety of situations, they tend to get told and retold. Nothing wears out from use faster than a story.

A Kind of Humor for People Who Like to Get Even: Improbable Images

A second form of effective humor consists of improbable images. It involves comparisons (generally using the word "like") that are unflattering. This kind of humor is especially useful in characterizing adversely people and proposals you don't like. It's a humorous approach you can use yourself, without poring over joke books.

Donald, Dolly, and Roseanne: Always There Whether We Need Them or Not

For example, suppose you're criticizing a proposal that your industry take a step you believe is out of character. You could say, "It would be like Donald Trump writing a book entitled: *My Life: A Study in Humility.*"

Or suppose you're describing a merger of mismatched companies. "It was a little like watching Luciano Pavarotti sing a duet with Roseanne (Barr) Arnold. It wasn't a pretty sight."

Or consider the insurance executive who was responding negatively to the suggestion that his company offer health insurance for pets. He thought the idea would generate a lot of window-shoppers, but not many buyers. He said, "It would be like having Dolly Parton enter the pole vault at the Olympics. You'd probably fill the stands, but you wouldn't see any records broken."

There are a lot of things (and many people, including Dolly, Roseanne, and The Donald) in life that seem to be intrinsically funny. Mention their names, and audiences chuckle. You may want to look at them as "humor lifelines" if your presentations are drowning in a sea of solemnity.

When the Laugh's on You: Self-Deprecation

A third form of humor is self-deprecation. Individuals who are self-confident enough to poke fun at themselves can establish good bonds with an audience. RJR Nabisco CEO Lewis Gerstner reportedly said he was "first in [his] army cooking class." This kind of humor is a sign of an individual with enough self-assurance to make fun of himself.

Self-deprecation works best when the speaker has attained a higher status than that of the audience: a CEO speaking to employees, a President speaking to Congress, a general in the armed services speaking to other officers, a business manager speaking to subordinates. Self-deprecation helps to establish the speaker as a "regular sort." This form of humor, however, isn't appropriate when the speaker has a lot to be deprecatory about. In other words, Queen Elizabeth can use it (but probably wouldn't). But if her footman makes a presentation, he probably shouldn't.

One individual who's used self-deprecation successfully is Ted Kelly, then a senior executive at Aetna. "As Irish as Paddy's pig," Kelly was brought up and educated near Dublin. Years of living in Canada and the United States (and gaining a Ph.D. at MIT) have not diminished his Irish brogue.

When he took over Aetna's largest business unit, he called a meeting of his managers. Some of them were nervous about possible changes in personnel. Kelly's opening comments were an attempt to break the ice.

Okay, as Long as It's Not that Damn Fuchsia!

In a deadpan tone, he informed the group that the rumors that the division would move from Connecticut to Ireland were "totally untrue." He added, "On the other hand, there's the question of Aetna's 'burnt orange' color. I think it would be nice if we changed it . . . to green . . . *Kelly* Green." The audience laughed, and the ice melted.

Two Other Examples of Self-Deprecation

Another talented individual who uses self-deprecation is Larry Wilson, CEO of Rohm & Haas. Right after he became chairman of the company, Wilson was asked by his alma mater, The Wharton School, to address its students. The topic was "Reflections of a New CEO."

Wilson contrasted the challenges he saw in his new job with the way he might look at them 20 years hence. He acknowledged that memory tends to cast a "golden haze" over the past. Wilson added that when we're young, we tend to focus on challenges. When we're older, we tend to emphasize (and perhaps *to embellish*) our accomplishments.

To illustrate his point, Wilson quoted the golfer Chi-Chi Rodriguez. When asked why he had been more successful on the senior golf tour than he had as a younger man on the regular tour, Rodriguez said, "Look, the older I *get*, the better I *was*."

Another executive quoted Harry Truman's assertion that "a leader is someone with the ability to get other people do what they don't want to do—and to like it."

He added, "If that's true, the real expert on leadership is . . . *my daughter*."

DO UNTO OTHERS . . . BUT GENTLY: DEPRECATION OF OTHERS

Self-deprecation is an important form of humor, and it's relatively easy to use. That differentiates it from my fourth form of humor, the *gentle* deprecation of others. The emphasis here is on the "gentle." No speaker wants to give offense, so there's some danger in this approach. If it's handled with tact and skill, however, it can be very effective.

The Math Nerd Who Busted Broncos

Jim Lynn, former CEO of Aetna, liked to use this approach, especially on occasions such as the retirement of fellow executive Gene Burton. The head of Aetna's health-benefits area, Burton seemed to the world the essence of an insurance executive. An actuary by training, Burton once posed for a poster/advertisement seeking to recruit college math majors for careers as actuaries. The ad featured Burton's benign countenance under the boldfaced heading MATH NERD.

In Lynn's remarks, he noted that Gene presented the "straightest" of images to the world. His secretary of 20 years said she'd never seen him in the office without his coat and tie. But, Lynn noted, there was another Gene Burton people never knew: the man who grew up on an Arizona ranch; the man who spent his spare moments in cowboy hats, boots,

and jeans, riding horses and roping steers; the mild-man-
nered mathematician who turned into a Dodge City poker
player when it came time to close a business deal.

Lynn captured the dichotomy between the Gene Burton
the world knew—the "public man"—and the vastly different
"private man."

The gentle kidding of others can transcend humor and
become a form of real affection. When it does so, it reflects
well on both the speaker and the recipient of the gentle
joshing.

DO NEW YORK CABBIES AND TRAFFIC JAMS
DISPROVE DARWIN'S THEORY?
LIFE'S ABSURDITIES

A fifth form of humor involves outlining "life's little
absurdities." We all ride in taxis with drivers who don't speak
English and aren't familiar with local geography. We all
stand in line at the motor vehicle office, waiting our turn to
be insulted. We all sit in traffic jams that are as endless as
they are irritating.

In addition, we all confront teenagers who assure us
that our experience and wisdom count for naught in today's
world. We all wrestle with IRS forms dedicated to the principle of incomprehensibility. We all work at some point for
individuals who seem unaware not only of our potential, but
also of our very existence.

In other words, we all encounter absurdity. As much as
this can be a cause of irritation in life, it can be a rich source
of humor in presentations. To share our experience of absurdity is to share our humanity.

That's precisely what Ron Compton, Aetna CEO, did in
a speech to an audience made up mainly of computer
specialists. He talked about the widely held view that non-
specialists feared technology and wouldn't use it unless
ordered to do so.

Did You Ever Meet an ATM You Didn't Like?

"Don't believe it," Compton said. He illustrated his point by referring to the rise of Automatic Teller Machines (ATMs) at banks. He noted the ATMs' popularity occurred despite predictions that bank customers would revolt against the loss of "personal service."

He observed: "Remember that 'personal service'? Remember standing in those long lines to cash a check for $50?" At this point, Compton's audience began to chuckle.

He continued: "And remember what that teller looked— and acted—like? (At this reference, many in the audience laughed.)

Compton said, "Remember the stern look you'd get from the teller? Remember the suspicious look *your check* got—as if it were a holdup note in code? (The audience was laughing more loudly, and many people were applauding.)

"And then," he said, "the teller would start slowly dialing one of those old rotary phones to see if you had enough money in your account to cover the check."

He concluded, "And that's why people will stand out in the cold—even in the pouring rain—to use the automatic teller machines. They remember that 'personal service' back in the bank, and they never want to confront that teller again."

The audience howled. Compton had touched a major "hot button," the one labeled Experiences We'd Like to Avoid Repeating.

In Our Battle Against the Indignities of Modern Life, Guess Who's Winning the War?

When used well in presentations, humor humanizes presentations. It says, for example, "like you, I have grown older—although not wiser—waiting for my number to come up as I stood in line at the Motor Vehicle Bureau." It tells the audience the speaker is a fellow combatant against the indignities of modern existence—a battle whose outcome is, at best, uncertain.

Points to Remember:

- Use humor wisely, and it can be an important tool in winning the interest and support of your audience.

- Aim to evoke a smile or a chuckle, rather than a belly laugh.

- Rely on practice and "trial runs" to sharpen your skill in using humor.

- Experiment with using the five most effective forms of presentational humor:
  - all-weather jokes or stories
  - improbable images
  - self-deprecation
  - gentle deprecation of others
  - recitations of "life's little absurdities."

11

THE Q AND A: MAKE IT MORE "A" THAN "Q"

The successful conduct of a question-and-answer period depends on the speaker's deft dominance of the session.

WHO "OWNS" THE Q & A?

Good presentations result from solid preparation. The speaker should craft every aspect of what's said so as to get the audience to respond favorably to the call to action. But when there's a question-and-answer (Q & A) period, a presentation extends beyond its formal boundaries.

The Q & A should be an extension of the basic presentation. The easiest Q & A sessions are those when the requests are for information or clarification alone. The audience asks questions and the speaker provides answers.

It's a different matter with presentations that raise significant issues, perhaps controversial ones. In that case, the Q & A may result in the speaker having to depend on ideas raised in the presentation. Some of the "questions" may in fact be short speeches outlining the supposed questioner's viewpoint on issues. In rare cases, the Q & A might surface "show offs" in the audience, people seeking to demonstrate their expertise on subjects.

It's essential to keep in mind that presenters are guests. They were invited so the audience could hear their information and ideas. The presentation belongs to the speaker, and so does the question period. For that reason, the Q & A offers presenters opportunities to reinforce the points they made in their previous remarks.

IN THE Q & A, THE BEST SURPRISE . . . IS NO SURPRISE

If a speaker has given a provocative, challenging presentation, there should be many good questions. But none of the questions should come as a true surprise.

An essential part of a speaker's preparation should be to anticipate questions and prepare answers for them. Questions do not really come "out of the blue." Whatever your subject, there are only a finite number of questions. Most of them are predictable, including the ones you'd least like to hear.

THE PRIMACY OF THE PRESENTERS

In good presentations, speakers do not cede control of the Q & A to the audience. They don't let aggressive questioners take over control of the meeting. They don't let "questioners" use the Q & A as an opportunity to make their own speeches. Most of all, they don't let themselves be surprised—knocked off balance—by unexpected questions.

In this chapter, you'll learn how to keep control of a Q & A—to make it serve your purposes. Questioners don't always play fair. They may want to lead you far afield from the subjects you want to discuss.

"WELCOME TO THE MINE FIELD"

If you're a public figure (an elected official, for example), they may want to trip you up, to force you to answer embarrassing questions, even to make you look bad. If they disagree with the point of view you're espousing, they may want to distract you from your primary message.

FOUR THINGS THAT GO WRONG IN Q & As

Q & As generally fail for the same reason that presentations do: lack of preparation. First, speakers neglect to think about—and prepare answers to—the difficult questions their presentations might evoke.

Second, presenters allow themselves to be trapped by "loaded" questions.

Third, they fail to control persistent questioners who are using the Q & A as an attempt to seize the limelight.

Finally, they allow themselves to be distracted by trivial or irrelevant questions, and thus they fail to reinforce the points they've made in their formal presentations.

As a result of these failures, they're hesitant, discursive, and stumbling in their answers.

Let's look at these failings one by one and suggest ways presenters can overcome them.

FAILING #1: NEGLECTING TO ANTICIPATE QUESTIONS AND PREPARE SUITABLE ANSWERS

This is a fundamental flaw. It can undermine the speaker's credibility, even with a basically friendly, supportive audience. A poor performance in the Q & A will shift authority to the questioner, who will seem to have thought more deeply about the subject, to know more about it.

If the audience is skeptical or hostile toward the speaker's point of view, a poorly handled Q & A can be even more disastrous. We've all seen it on television news shows like "Meet the Press" or "Crossfire": The "guest" gives a poor or evasive answer to a question. The questioners probe, the guest continues to evade, and the questioning becomes progressively more hostile. The guest either becomes ever more defensive or, worse, blurts out something unfortunate.

LACK OF PREPARATION: TED KENNEDY GETS "MUDD" IN HIS EYE

In some cases, lack of preparation can have disastrous consequences. Take the example of Ted Kennedy in the period before the 1980 election. Jimmy Carter was the sitting Democratic President, and Kennedy decided to oppose him. Many experts thought he would present a serious challenge to the incumbent. But it never happened.

The Kennedy campaign was derailed, in large part, by one disastrous, televised interview. It was conducted by Roger Mudd, who asked Kennedy a question that historian Theodore H. White said should have been "an opening to any candidate for a long base hit, if not a home run." Mudd's question was: "Senator Kennedy, why do you think you'd be a good President?"

Kennedy gave Mudd a startled look, and then he said the following: "Well, I'm—were I to—make the announcement . . . is because I have a great belief in this country, that it is—has—more natural resources than any other nation in the world . . . the greatest technology of any country in the world . . . . And the energy and the resourcefulness of this nation, I think, should be focused on these problems in a way that brings a sense of restoration in this country by its people to . . . And I would basically feel that—it's imperative for the country to either move forward . . . that it can't stand still . . . or otherwise it will move back."

Why Is This Man Running?
Answer: Dynastic Considerations

Kennedy's response to Mudd was embarrassing. It's as if he was frantically searching his mind for the right clichés. It contains factual inaccuracies; for example, the United States does not have more natural resources than any other country. (That honor goes to the Soviet Union.) The reference to "a sense of restoration" (of the Kennedy dynasty?) is offensive. The hemming and hawing in the answer makes it seem as if Kennedy lacks a clear idea of why he is asking the American people to support him.

Campaign historian (and Kennedy family friend) Theodore White characterizes the Mudd interview as "a disaster" for the Senator's presidential aspirations.

What if Ted Kennedy had said the following? "Mr. Mudd, I want to be the President of the United States because I can work with the Congress to help this nation reach its great potential. As a nation, we have abundant resources. We have sophisticated technology. Most of all, we have a resourceful and resilient people. What we need now is the leadership and vision to turn this nation's great promise into great achievement. I'm running for President because I believe I can provide that leadership and that vision."

If Kennedy had said that, would the history of the 1980s have been different? We'll never know. Why didn't he give a better answer to Mudd's question? It's simple: He hadn't prepared a good answer.

A CONTRASTING EXAMPLE: REAGAN IN 1984

In contrast to Kennedy's performance, during a televised debate with Walter Mondale in 1984, Ronald Reagan's response to a question was what may have kept him *in* the White House. Reagan was being hurt at the time by the "Age Issue," the fact that he was the oldest individual ever elected to the presidency. Reagan had aggravated his problems in this regard by giving some vague, rambling answers to questions in the first debate.

Pat Caddell Passes on the Kinder, Gentler Approach

Exploiting the "age issue" was a vital part of Mondale's strategy for the second debate. Patrick Caddell, Democratic pollster and Mondale advisor, had written a confidential memo to the Mondale campaign pointing to the age issue as Reagan's albatross. Caddell had said, "As a 73-year-old conservative ideologue, Reagan is in the difficult position of proving that he has a grasp of the future, a plan for it, or a stake in it."

Caddell had added, "The overriding objective of the [second] debate must be to 'break' Reagan—hurt him on age, on his lack of knowledge, on his grasp of issues."

The Reagan camp was worried about the second debate. The President practiced assiduously. In his extended rehearsals for the debate, Reagan enlisted the aid of syndicated columnist George Will. That journalist joined others in asking Reagan hard questions. By the time the second debate arrived, Reagan was very familiar with the kinds of questions the journalists/panelists would ask—and had good answers ready.

The debate proceeded. Eventually, Henry Trewhitt of the Baltimore *Sun* addressed a question to Reagan about the "age issue." Trewhitt said: "You are already the oldest President in history. . . . President Kennedy had to go for days on end with very little sleep during the Cuban missile crisis. Is there any doubt in your mind that you would be able to function under such circumstances?"

With Mondale primed to exploit the "age issue," there seemed no way Reagan could answer the question to his advantage.

Old Dog Teaches Younger One New Trick

Reagan's advisors may have thought the same thing, so they had primed him with an unusual answer to the question. Reagan said: "Not at all, Mr. Trewhitt, and I want you to know that also I will not make age an issue of this campaign."

Reagan then looked at Mondale, a man in his mid-50s who had served one term as Vice President and several terms as a U.S. Senator, and said, "I am not going to exploit for political purposes *my opponent's* youth and inexperience."

The audience erupted in laughter. Even Mondale laughed, perhaps more in sorrow than in humor. He may have realized that his presidential campaign had cratered on the Reagan quip. In the November election, Mondale carried only his home state of Minnesota and the District of Columbia. Reagan won the electoral votes of 49 states.

FAILING #2: ALLOWING YOURSELF TO BE TRAPPED BY "LOADED" QUESTIONS

The questions Roger Mudd asked Kennedy and Trewhitt asked Reagan were not "loaded." They were not designed to damage the position of the person questioned. They dealt with valid issues in which there was real public interest. True loaded questions are designed to embarrass presenters, to put them on the defensive, to make them look bad. The classic loaded question is "When did you stop beating your spouse?" The more subtle version is: "How's your recovery program for spousal abuse going?"

Most presenters will encounter this situation rarely, if at all. It deals with individuals who fire one question after another at you, usually with little interest in your answers. Chronic questioners usually appear at well-attended public meetings, where they can have a large audience for their antics. They're looking for a chance to dominate the meeting, to get their "15 minutes" of celebrity. They're not really interested in your answers to their questions. Rather, they want to get your goat, to make you flustered and angry.

As Dr. Jerry Tarver says of Q & As, the best approach is to be "unfailingly polite." In other words, don't lose your temper at loaded questions. Instead, refuse to answer such questions—but don't let the questioner know that's what you're doing.

Don't Get Angry; Instead, Rephrase the Question

I worked for oil companies during the energy crises of the 1970s and 1980s. These companies were drilling offshore wells in sensitive areas. In one case, a company I worked for had a major well "blow out" in the North Sea, causing millions of gallons of oil to flow into the water. As you might imagine, a lot of people asked hard questions of our executives. Sometimes the questions were more than "loaded." They were downright nasty.

For example, the following question: "Isn't it true you guys are more interested in making obscene profits than in protecting our precious water supply?" This is not a question demanding an answer; it's an accusation demanding an apology. The question boils down to: "Aren't you guys a bunch of greedy polluters?"

If an apology is in order, make it. If it's not, don't try to answer the question/accusation. To answer a loaded question is to accept it as valid. A better approach to loaded questions is to rephrase them. That means to interpret and modify the question so that you can answer it in a way that serves your purposes.

For example, faced with a "greedy polluter" type of question, you should say: "Your question deals with our policy toward environmental protection." Then discuss your environmental policies—and accomplishments—in crisp, clear terms. This approach "defangs" the question and allows you to answer on your terms, not on the hostile questioner's.

"Ask and You Shall Not Receive": The Case of Hubert H. Humphrey

The late Senator from Minnesota liked to talk, and he appeared frequently on "Meet the Press" and other network interview shows. He never answered loaded questions. He rarely answered valid, "unloaded" questions. Instead, he went on the shows with a set idea of what he wanted to say. What he gave the interviewers and the TV audience was a speech masquerading as a Q & A.

Reporters would ask him how the nation could pay for some of the social programs Humphrey advocated. He'd say something like: "How, as a humane and caring nation, can we do otherwise?" Then he would launch into a graphic discussion of poverty and infant mortality.

Reporters would sometimes remonstrate with Humphrey that he hadn't answered their questions. He'd nod and then launch into another part of his prepared script. The news panelists were helpless before the onslaught of Senator Humphrey's oratory. They were like traffic cops trying to enforce speed limits at the Indianapolis 500.

Humphrey's approach was extreme. Yet he understood that, as the guest, it was his message that counted. He appeared on the interview shows not to satisfy the newspeople's curiosity about how he'd answer their questions; he appeared to advance his views. He was there to win converts—and votes—not to make debating points.

A Man with a Singular Message: "Don't Steal This Book. Buy It"

In any presentation, you should always keep your purpose—the result you want—foremost in your mind. For example, the author of a book on health and fitness for young people appeared on the "Sonya Live" interview program on CNN. The author's purpose could be summed up in three words: "Buy My Book."

The hostess and her callers asked the author various questions. For most respondents, the temptation might be to turn into a freestanding expert, in this case, a guru on health and fitness. This gentleman resisted the temptation. Whenever he was asked a question, he referred to his book: "School lunches? Well, I've devoted an entire chapter of my book to that question." He then delivered a short summary of the point his book made.

Another caller asked him if there was a "relationship between school grades and nutrition?" His reply was, "There's a direct correlation." He stated what the correlation was and concluded, "I urge you to read my discussion about this matter in the book."

This gentleman recognized *his* purpose for being on "Sonya Live." He wanted people to buy his book. Every answer he gave was directed toward that end. He was on the program to provide information insofar as it served his sales purpose.

FAILING #3: NEGLECTING TO CONTROL PERSISTENT QUESTIONERS WHO TRY TO "HOG" THE MEETING

Annual meetings of shareholder-owned companies seem to attract persistent questioners. In fact, there are a number of individuals who travel from one annual meeting to another. They generally try to dominate the question period, asking the corporate CEO one question after another. For these so-called "gadflies," the chance to hold the chairman's feet to the fire is the high point of their existence. Their insistent questions often take a hostile or mocking tone.

Most people at annual meetings are either corporate employees or long-term shareholders. They generally support the views of corporate management and resent the tone and quantity of the gadflies' questions. Sometimes they boo or even try to shout down the loquacious critics of management. These actions tend only to encourage the gadflies, who after all are usually trying to call attention to themselves by tweaking the CEO's nose.

What's the Answer . . . in Dealing with People Who Want Attention More than Answers?

Stick to your guns. Don't allow the questioner to start a dialogue. Answer the person's question (singular), and then turn your eyes away from that individual and call on another questioner. If the gadfly is truly obnoxious and persists in shouting out questions, say something like, "You've had your turn. Please be fair and let other people have theirs."

The "Out to Lunch" Tactic

What happens when no one else has questions and the gadfly still demands attention? At one corporation where I worked we always had one or more gadflies at annual meetings, which were held from 10:30 A.M. until noon. One effective device the CEO used was to look at his watch and announce that, since only one person had questions, he was going to adjourn the meeting so the people present could have lunch. However, he indicated, he and his staff would stay to respond to any remaining questions.

The gadfly vainly protested this tactic. And when the meeting ended, the only people remaining in the room were the CEO and his staff. Since the gadfly was looking for attention rather than answers, he, too, was soon literally, as well as figuratively, out to lunch.

If the timing of your meeting doesn't allow you to be saved by the lunch bell, ask the audience if only one person has remaining questions. If so, announce that you're adjourning the meeting (so that everyone can get back to work or home or wherever), but that you will be available to answer any questions that remain. Take my word for it: Your persistent questioner will disappear as soon as the audience leaves.

THE GENERALS AND THE GULF WAR: A STUDY IN THE USE OF Q & A TO ADVANCE A CAUSE

One of the best examples of using Q & A effectively was by the U.S. armed forces during the Gulf War. This conflict made household names out of three formerly little-known generals: Colin Powell, head of the Joint Chiefs of Staff; General Thomas W. Kelly, who delivered the daily 3 P.M. briefings; and General Norman Schwarzkopf, commander of the coalition forces in the Persian Gulf.

General Powell presented the hard-nosed, competent side of the military, particularly with his "cut it off . . . and kill it" description of U.S. military strategy in regard to the Iraqi army.

The press later revealed that Powell's statement about cutting and killing definitely was not an ad lib. In fact, he had developed it in discussion with his aides and advisors. They considered whether it was too brutal and decided the wording reflected resolution and confidence.

The Wit and Wisdom of General Tom Kelly

A somewhat kinder and gentler side of the war was represented by General Thomas Kelly. He revealed himself to be a witty, informed, likable individual. He showed how the use of calculated humor could play a role in presenting the military effort in a positive light.

For example, one reporter asked him how the military could justify sending a squadron of B-52s to bomb a single SCUD missile site. Kelly replied, "My opinion is that's a delightful way to kill a fly."

Later, after the ground war ended with Iraqi troops in disarray, a reporter was concerned that American soldiers might still be in danger. He asked Kelly to characterize the relationship between U.S. troops and the Iraqis. Without missing a beat, Kelly said, "Have you ever seen a cat waiting outside a mouse hole?"

Kelly's Performance: A Tribute to Preparation and Personality

After the Gulf War ended, Kelly discussed how he prepared for his news conferences, which occurred every day at 3 P.M. He and his aides would get together at 7 A.M. to discuss developments in the war. They would also discuss which members of the media would be present at the 3 P.M. briefing. Then they would seek to identify questions they might expect and which answers would be appropriate.

"Good on His Feet?" Guess Again!

Kelly's briefing demonstrated a key point about Q & As: The more thinking you do on your "seat," the better you'll do on your feet. Hamlet was on target when he said, "The readiness is all." Preparation is all.

The Case of Norman Schwarzkopf:
Using the Q & A to Make Policy . . .
and to Make War

General Norman Schwarzkopf conducts a Q & A the way Leonard Bernstein conducted a symphony orchestra—with great skill and inimitable style. As with Bernstein, Schwarzkopf leaves no doubt about who's in charge. In the face of the General's dominating personality, seasoned war correspondents take on the demeanor of obedient school children. In handling questions as in conducting military operations, Schwarzkopf exemplifies what the military calls "command and control."

Thoughtful Answers to Tough Questions

Schwarzkopf is a man in control not only of his troops, but of his answers to media inquiries. For example, before the Gulf War, a reporter asked him whether he was "a hawk or a dove." Schwarzkopf's response showed he had anticipated the question. He said, "I don't consider myself dovish, and I certainly don't consider myself hawkish. I'd describe myself as owlish—that is, wise enough to understand that you do everything possible to avoid war." (This highly quotable remark illustrates the careful calculation underlying the General's answer.)

The Q & A as an Instrument of Policy:
Sending a Message to Saddam Hussein

Schwarzkopf used his interviews and press briefings to advance U.S. policy. He also used them to engage in a tactic as old as warfare itself, what the Greeks called "the epic brag"; taunting one's enemy. It's a technique designed to bring one's antagonist down to size, to belittle him, and to intimidate him.

Schwarzkopf realized that Saddam Hussein, like the rest of the world, was "watching CNN." Thus, many of Schwarzkopf's "answers" to questions were really messages directed to Saddam Hussein.

Some reporters picked up on this tactic. In a briefing given after the start of the air war, a reporter observed, "General, you've referred today and on previous occasions to Saddam in personal terms." The reporter continued, "Do you think Saddam is listening to your words now, and are you trying to psychologically intimidate him?"

Schwarzkopf replied, "I've been trying to psychologically intimidate him from long before the beginning of the conflict, [and] I sincerely hope he knows what's going on."

Get Beyond His Homicidal Tendencies, and Saddam Is Quite a Guy

Schwarzkopf's most famous public comment was in response to a question about how he viewed Saddam Hussein's military leadership. The General said, "As far as Saddam Hussein being a great military strategist . . . he is neither a strategist . . . nor is he schooled in the operational art . . . nor is he a tactician . . . nor is he a general." Schwarzkopf added, "Nor is he a soldier."

He concluded, "Other that that, he's a great military man."

The press conference at which he made this memorable statement became known as "the mother of all briefings," an ironic play on Saddam's hyperbolic assertion that the Gulf War would be "the mother of all battles."

A good part of Schwarzkopf's fame derives from his superb performance in this Q & A session. His success illustrates that question and answer periods can be much more than a mere formality following a presentation. In skilled hands, the Q & A can support and supplement a speaker's themes and call to action.

CRANDALL OF AMERICAN AIRLINES: A PERFECT "10" ON A Q & A

One of the best ways to improve your ability to handle Q & A is to study the work of masters like Schwarzkopf. Pay particular attention to published versions of Q & As where the respondents (or the institutions they represent) are "under fire."

One example that's worth looking up is the Q & A *Time* conducted with Robert Crandall, CEO of American Airlines. It appeared in the October 28, 1991, edition (pages 18 and 22).

The *Time* interviewer took an accusatory approach, charging that airline deregulation had failed, saddling passengers with fewer flights, higher fares, and less comfort. Crandall obviously was well prepared for the interview.

For example, the interviewer asserts that "deregulation has backfired, that it has enriched the biggest airlines [and] has hurt passengers by producing less competition, higher fares, and fewer choices.

Crandall's answer: "It would be hard to be more wrong. Studies by the Brookings Institution show that during the first 10 years of deregulation passengers saved $1 billion."

Later, the questioner asks, "What about concerns that the financial stress of deregulation has hurt safety?"

Crandall's reply: "Anyone who says that is wrong. The FAA is responsible for safety. Safety was not deregulated. The safety record of the airline industry is materially and dramatically better than it was during regulation."

Again, the Crandall interview is worth studying. In bluntly eloquent terms, Crandall reiterates his point that deregulation is good for consumers and good for the airlines. He fends off tough (and sometimes unfair) questions with crisp, direct, informed answers. His performance is a model for anyone seeking to handle questions well.

Points to Remember:

- Control your Q & A sessions—it's your presentation and your Q & A.
- Anticipate questions you'll get and prepare answers for them in advance.
- Use the Q & A to advance the arguments you made in your presentation and to reiterate your call to action.
- Keep your answers short (30 seconds or less) and to the point.
- Interpret and restate questions so that you can answer them in ways that serve *your* purposes.
- Don't allow questions (especially hostile ones) to start a dialogue; they deserve an answer, not a platform for their views.
- Study the way "the masters" (Schwarzkopf, Crandall, and others) handle the Q & A, and emulate their examples.

12

WRITE A SPEECH FOR THE BOSS? YES, YOU CAN!

SONNETS IN SANSKRIT, FABLES IN FARSI

Ask the average people if they could write a speech for someone else and they will react as if you'd asked them to produce a sonnet in Sanskrit or a fable in Farsi. But if you can produce an acceptable speech for yourself, you can do one for someone else.

THE MAKING OF A SPEECH WRITER

Let me tell you about a person I'll call "Mickey." I've changed the name of this individual, but his story is true in every detail. When I worked in the oil industry, Mickey called and asked if he could talk to me. He said he knew that, like him, I'd been a college teacher of English. He'd heard that corporate speech writers made a lot more money than English professors. How, he asked, could he become a speech writer?

I gave him some background materials and an assignment: to write a speech about how gasoline was really a bargain. (Most Americans in those "energy crisis" days thought it was a colossal "rip off.") Mickey went off and wrote the speech. It wasn't great, but it was decent. We paid him $500 for his efforts and told him we'd call on him again.

A month later, we did call Mickey. He was out of town, in Dallas, interviewing for a job as a speech writer with Diamond Shamrock. They offered him the job. But he turned them down to take a better paying job as a speech writer with a bigger company in Pennsylvania.

Being a Speech Writer: You Have to Go Around Only Once

When he accepted the speech writing job, Mickey had written one speech. But two major companies viewed him (correctly, in my view) as a speech writer! In other words, write a speech, and you're a speech writer.

After Mickey joined corporate America, I lost track of him for a while. When Aetna was recruiting me to work there, I found out that my main competitor for the job had been . . . Mickey. I got the job, which was only fair considering that it had been my magic wand that had transformed Mickey into a speech writer.

MY SON STEPHEN, THE SPEECH WRITER

I became a speech writer in 1977, which of course was the year in which I wrote my first formal speech. More accurately, I became a speech *consultant.* Let me explain the difference.

My first boss took me aside and gave me some advice. "Look, Steve," he said, "I wouldn't say much in public about being the chairman's scribe. Most people think the chairman works day and night putting together remarks." He added, "The chances of the CEO's scribe having the title 'speech writer' on a business card are about the same as someone having a card with the phrase 'Chairman's Mistress.' "

At that instant, I transformed myself from a speech *writer* to a speech *consultant.* That's important to keep in mind when you become a speech writer—that is, when you write one speech. The person you write it for will be grateful and will undoubtedly ask you to write more of them. But he or she won't be grateful if you come out of the shadows, pointing to yourself and proclaiming, "That's my speech. I wrote it." In other words, be a speech *consultant,* not a speech *writer.*

In recent decades, speech writers have become less anonymous. A few have become famous: authors and lecturers Richard Goodwin and Ted Sorenson (speech writers for John F. Kennedy); *New York Times* columnist William Safire and author Ben Stein (speech writers for Richard Nixon); author James Fallows and *New Republic* editor Hendrik Hertzberg (speech writers for Jimmy Carter); and author Peggy Noonan (speech writer for Ronald Reagan).

For every famous speech writer, however, there are a thousand who labor in anonymity. (Don't feel sorry for them, however. Even some of the anonymous ones are very highly paid—up to $150,000 per year.) Moreover, for every full-time speech writer, there are hundreds who write speeches part time.

Surprise: The Executives Get the "Perks"

As a general rule, the higher up in an organization a person is, the more likely he (or, much less frequently, she) will have the services of a speech writer. This fact shocks some people. They wonder, "Why can't those guys write their own speeches, the way I have to do?"

There are two answers: one, life isn't fair; two, to prepare one major speech (and get it "approved" by the Big Guy's staff) might take as much as 40 or 50 hours. Most heads of organizations don't have that much time to devote to a speech, particularly when they may be giving several presentations a week.

SO *THAT'S* WHAT DELEGATION MEANS

Someday, somewhere you'll be asked to write a speech for a "higher-up" in your organization. "Oh, by the way, Johnson, would you put together a 20-minute speech for J.B. He's going to speak to the local Chamber of Commerce. And could I see a draft by a week from Tuesday?"

Invariably, the request will come from your boss—call her "B.J."—and J.B. will be her boss. (In fact, J.B. probably asked B.J. to produce the speech. Since you report to B.J., the honor falls to you. That's what managers mean by the word "delegation.")

Remember the Cartoon Where the Boss Called
In the Subordinate and Said,
"I've Decided You're Ready for Additional
Responsibility, so I've Decided to Blame
Something Really Big on You?"

The boss has "honored" you. She's offered you a chance to become "highly visible," to write a speech for J.B., whom you've never met, rarely seen, and perhaps never heard speak a single word.

That is, B.J., your boss, has set you up, if not for failure, at least for frustration. Why is that so? Because she's given you a mystery assignment. She hasn't told you anything of value. She hasn't told you what J.B. wants to talk about—let alone offered you a chance to meet with the Big Boss to find out. She hasn't told you anything about the audience: what they know about the "subject" (whatever it may be) and how they might respond to J.B.'s ideas (whatever they are).

"Be Sure to Tell Me How
the Suicide Mission Goes, Johnson"

B.J. hasn't given you a speech assignment. She's given you a live land mine. After she does so, she'll invariably pick up some papers on her desk and appear to be intensely interested in their contents. She's hoping you'll go back to your desk and, by some miracle, turn out a speech that will be acceptable to J.B. Fat chance!

Make Your Boss a Co-conspirator, or, It's Always Nice to Have Company When Walking Through a Mine Field

Don't let your boss off the hook. Refuse to slink out of the office. Tear her away from her papers. Make her a co-conspirator. Remind her (subtly) that her career, like yours, may be riding on the success of the speech.

Launch the co-conspiracy by getting from her every scrap of specific information she has about the speech request. Which individual from which group invited J.B.? Did this person indicate why they wanted J.B. as a speaker? And why did J.B. accept this particular invitation?

Also, get your boss's thinking on: Which individuals in the company might provide information for use in the remarks; which people should see drafts of the remarks before they go to the Big Boss; what materials (previous speeches, economic studies, financial statistics, articles, books, and so forth) exist that could provide grist for the presentation.

Ask to See J.B., Unless His Last Name Really Happens to Be "Medusa"

Finally, tell (don't ask) your boss that you want to speak with J.B. about the speech. Put this demand in a positive light; tell her it only makes sense to talk to the Big Boss in order to make sure you include the points near and dear to J.B.'s heart. (Take into account that your boss might not want you to be all that visible to J.B., who might think *she's* writing the speech.)

J.B. Will Be Out for the Next
Three-and-a-Half Months

However, J.B. himself might not want to see you. Why? Because your presence might remind him he's committed to make a presentation that he'd rather forget about until the last minute.

Before you leave your boss's office, get her commitment to try to get you in to see J.B. (Suggest that "of course" your boss might want to tag along; she'll probably say, "Thanks, but no thanks" because she knows a mine field when she sees one.)

Don't Worry Overmuch About J.B.'s "Style"

When you get back to your office, your mind will be racing. Like most beginning speech writers you'll worry, with some justification, about how to capture the speaker's style.

However, don't set yourself the impossible task of trying to make the speech sound exactly like the speaker. Instead, set yourself a more achievable goal: to make your speech draft one that will get the speaker purring contentedly.

In writing for J.B., you'd want to include (if appropriate to the occasion) one of his pet stories or anecdotes. To the degree possible, you'd want to include his favorite themes, ideas, and—especially—his pet phrases. For instance, if J.B. always says "There's nothing wrong with business that lower interest rates won't cure," then say so.

In other words, try to find out what J.B. "always says," and then put it in his speech. (Ron Compton of Aetna liked to talk about making the company "quick, flexible, and right." The phrase appeared in nearly every presentation he made. Bill Douce of Phillips liked the words "vigorous" and "optimistic" in his remarks.)

The more of J.B. you get into his prepared remarks, the more acceptable—even brilliant—he'll find the presentation.

What If the Speaker Would Rather Eat Glass than See the Speech Writer?

The best way to find out what speakers want to say is to ask them. But what if the "client" absolutely refuses to see the speech writer? This is a sign that the speaker either (1) regrets having accepted the invitation and doesn't want even to think about it; or (2) regards either the event or the speech writer as unworthy of attention.

In this case, the writer should try to get the speaker's indirect involvement. One way to do this is to get the person who gave you the assignment to sit down with the client and discuss possible themes and ideas.

Then send the outline to the speaker and ask for approval of the direction you suggest. It's important to get your clients' involvement. Otherwise, you might find them regarding your draft with the same enthusiasm they'd manifest if someone had deposited on their desks half-eaten Big Macs.

A meeting with the speaker *is* highly desirable. But it's not absolutely essential. Even if you are able to get a meeting, you should try to find out everything you can about the speaker's habits and preferences, as well as the audience's make-up and attitudes.

I'll illustrate the steps you should take by discussing what went into preparing a specific presentation.

THE SPEECH I WROTE FOR LEE IACOCCA

I once wrote a speech for Lee Iacocca. I've never met Lee Iacocca, nor have I spoken to him on the phone. I've also never sent him an outline or asked the executive recruiter who gave me the assignment to discuss the speech with Iacocca.

The Director of Communications at Chrysler assured me those steps would not be necessary. Those were the days when Mr. Iacocca was firing speech writers at a rate of about one every six months. So perhaps the Chrysler PR people didn't want me to see "Mr. I" because they feared he wouldn't like my looks.

Working under such restrictions, I probably should have refused the assignment. Why didn't I? Because I needed the ridiculously large sum Chrysler offered to pay me for the speech, an offer that may have reflected Chrysler's perception about the difficulty of writing acceptably for the Great Man.

THE IACOCCA EVERYBODY KNOWS

Chrysler's PR department notwithstanding, Mr. Iacocca is not a hard person for whom to write. In fact, if you think about it, we all know a lot about Lee Iacocca's conversational style. We've seen him on interviews and, especially, in Chrysler ads. His autobiography (*Iacocca*, written in vintage Iacocca-ese by ghostwriter *par excellence* William Novak) is one of the most-read books of our time.

THE QUINTESSENCE OF BLUNTNESS

Iacocca's conversational style is nothing if not blunt. He's extremely colloquial (referring not to short-order cooks, for example, but to "hamburger flippers" and not to auto executives but to "car guys").

Iacocca speaks more like an auto union official than like the CEO of a major auto company (or "car company," as Iacocca would put it). His tone alternates between earnest evangelism for the domestic auto industry and sarcasm about his industry's critics and politicians. It's true that he "speaks his mind." But to be candid, his mind generally doesn't extend far beyond parochial "car business" concerns and "America First" economic jingoism.

We Know His "Beef," But Not His Brief for Action

Iacocca's speeches have one fundamental flaw. Invariably, they offer criticisms but don't provide workable solutions. In my terms, they don't really have a "call to action."

Iacocca tells us what he doesn't like: high interest rates that discourage people from buying cars; a worldwide auto market that gives Japanese exporters an advantage, that doesn't provide "a level playing field" for U.S. automakers; economists committed to "free trade" rather than "fair trade"; Washington politicians who are little more than blowhards; a health-care system that costs business too much; an educational system that's failing to teach people how to read and to do their numbers.

A Presentation Should Be More than Extended Grumbles

But what concrete solutions does he offer? He calls us not to action but to anger. It's not enough for speakers to make their presentations an extended grumble.

They have to tell us what to do about the deficiencies they discuss. Otherwise, such speakers just add to the prevailing national mood of negativism. They leave their audiences not only "concerned," but frustrated and directionless.

In a way, Iacocca's communications advisors have failed the man. They've assisted him in airing his complaints. But they haven't challenged him to take the next step: to advance a plan of action to overcome the deficiencies he sees in America. Thus, it may be that Iacocca as a spokesman for business is nothing more than a voice crying—and complaining—in the wilderness.

READ EVERYTHING;
TALK TO ANYONE WHO CAN HELP

Are my criticisms about Iacocca's presentations the result of sour grapes. No, they're the result of reading everything I could by—and about—him.

In doing a speech for someone else, take the same approach you would with a presentation you were doing. Find out everything you can about the audience (in this case, it was a national convention of realtors): their beliefs and attitudes; the issues facing their group; and the messages they've heard from previous speakers.

But of most importance, steep yourself in what the speaker has said previously. In this case, I read a number of Iacocca speeches on American business and the Japanese challenge and political and economic issues confronting American business.

Of even more importance, I sought out interviews that Iacocca had previously given. I didn't have any audio- or videotapes (which are especially useful when they're unedited). But I did have several newspaper and magazine interviews.

I scanned this material very carefully in order to determine what the football coaches call "tendencies." Specifically, I was looking for Iacocca's favorite ideas, words, and pet phrases, the locutions he turned to over and over again. For example, Iacocca loves the phrase "level playing field"; he uses it in reference to the supposed advantages that Japanese carmakers have in exporting automobiles to the United States.

Moreover, he enjoys scorning the experts who claimed that "services" in America were replacing the manufacturing sector. Iacocca's observation was that our society wasn't going to generate real wealth through "flipping hamburgers . . . and taking in each other's laundry."

Humble Beginnings Do Not Always Make a Humble Man

Finally, I read articles about Iacocca. Although this was the period when he was being lionized as the straight-shooting savior of American business, many of the pieces about him presented a mixed picture. They showed him as a man whose enormous achievements were matched by his equally enormous ego. He was arrogant and cocksure. He did not suffer fools gladly, and his definition of fools started with Henry Ford II and included everyone who disagreed with Iacocca.

To Know Them Is to Become Them

It's essential to know a lot about the person for whom you're writing. That's because, *in the act of writing, you have to do your best to become that individual.* It's a matter of learning how to inhabit the heart, mind, and vocal cords of your speaker. It helps me to look at the speaker as a character in a play I'm writing.

A presentation is not a "position paper." It's much more like dialogue—more accurately, a monologue—in a dramatic production. A presentation, like a play, shows a man or woman *speaking.* That's why a speech should sound like an individual talking, not like someone composing a master's thesis.

HOW'S YOUR "NEGATIVE CAPABILITY"?

Samuel Taylor Coleridge wrote about Shakespeare's capacity to become, for a time, one of his characters: Hamlet, Iago, Desdemona. He called it "negative capability." It's a form of losing oneself in another being. People who are utterly lacking in this capacity probably shouldn't write speeches for other people.

Here are a few samples from "my" Iacocca speech. For context, the remarks were made after the oil crisis of the early 1980s and the subsequent recession. In this section of the speech I quote, Iacocca is establishing the links between his business and that of the realtors:

What happened—what made our two industries so sick for so long? In five words, the economy went to hell. And all of us got burned.

We got hit with a one-two-three punch: the oil crisis, inflation, and high interest rates.

The oil crisis crashed into your business—and mine—like a freight train. In about seven years, a gallon of gasoline went from about 30 cents to a buck and a half.

Those oil-price hikes turned the car business on its head. We had to reengineer and retool to make cars smaller and more fuel efficient. At the same time, the boys in D.C. hit us with big bills for new regulations.

The energy crisis also flattened your business. Home buyers started having nightmares about gas and electric bills that looked like mortgage payments. So you're also "downsizing," with smaller homes and fewer "extras."

We saw the cost of living shoot through the roof. Interest rates went outa sight. All of a sudden—one day in 1980—we woke up to a prime rate that had gone over 21 percent. That tore the guts outa the housing business . . . and the car business. At those rates, a lot of buyers say: count me out..

A later section of the speech deals with a favorite subject of Iacocca's, the supposedly malevolent trade practices of Japanese auto makers (pardon me, "car makers"):

We're losing skilled, good-paying jobs. And the jobs we're creating are the ones where you wear a hat with a picture of Ronald McDonald . . . or where you walk around emptying the coin boxes of video games made in Japan.

Washington says, "Yeah, you've got a real problem, but if we do anything to help, we'd be violating some philosophy of free enterprise."

Bull. A theory that doesn't support American products . . . and American jobs . . . is a joke.

I'm damn tired of some politician reading me Adam Smith's comments about the invisible hand of the marketplace . . . while the Japanese car-makers are poking their thumbs in our eyes.

"Other than That, Mr. Iacocca, How'd You Like the Speech?"

How did Iacocca (and Chrysler) respond to this prepared speech? I never found out. And after reading about Mr. Iacocca and his habit of having speech writers for breakfast, I wasn't that interested in finding out.

Seriously, I found the experience of writing a speech for Lee Iacocca to be exhilarating—what the British call "jolly good fun." His freewheeling, "say anything" style was a challenge to mimic. It also marked a liberation from some of the buttoned-down corporate rhetoric I'd been producing for several years.

In "my" Iacocca speech I was able to make allusions to comments by individuals as disparate as former Communist Whittaker Chambers (who said: "history hit us like a freight train"); movie mogul Sam Goldwyn (who said: "include me out"); and speech writer Steve Maloney (who used the lines about the invisible hand and the thumb in the eye in a 1976 *Fortune* magazine article). With speeches, as with items like glass and paper, recycling is a must.

Points to Remember:

- Try hard to meet with your speakers to discuss what points they'd like to include in their speeches.

- Find out everything you can about the speaker, the audience, and the subject.
- Put your speakers into "their" speeches by injecting their favorite ideas, phrases, and words.
- Write for speakers as if they were characters in a play (or a "dramatic monologue").

13

THE PRELIMINARY ESSAY: FRAMEWORK FOR A PRESENTATION

When you have to write a speech (for yourself or some-one else), put it first in essay form . . . then edit it into a speech text. Follow this procedure even if you intend to make your presentation from notes or perhaps to "wing it."

If you decide to use a full speech text, it should be simpler, more colloquial, and clearer than your original essay. If you decide to use notes, they will be simpler—and leaner—than a speech text.

Let's look at the difference between essays, speeches, and notes.

WITH ESSAYS, YOU GO AROUND AS OFTEN AS YOU WANT; WITH PRESENTATIONS, "YOU GO AROUND ONLY ONCE"

In general, essayists seek to challenge their readers, to engage their minds, to stimulate thought about complex issues. They want their pieces to be read—and reread. With an essay, we can read a passage, reflect on it, and reread it, all at our leisure.

But with presentations (especially formal speeches), an audience doesn't get that luxury. We don't get a chance to rehear difficult or unclear passages. We either comprehend the remarks as they're delivered, or we don't. The words are spoken, and then they're gone.

Come Again?

At their best, essays and other forms of narrative writing challenge our intellects. As an example, consider some excerpts from Shirley Abbott's *The Bookmaker's Daughter*, a memoir about her father, both a bibliophile and a maker of "book" on horses.

Abbott says, "A father gives his daughter the sense of what her bargaining position with all men will be." She adds, "Ultimately, these bargains and all the others we learn to make within the family are called life."

The author's words are dense with significance. We need five minutes—or perhaps five years—to think about the meaning and implications of what Abbott says. As readers of her book, we have that time. If she were to speak the same sentences in a presentation, however, they would pass by so quickly that we could comprehend them only partially, if at all. Abbott's sentences are beautifully written, and deeply meaningful, but they would not be successful in a speech.

A FUNNY THING HAPPENED ON THE WAY TO THE SPEECH

In presentations, a speaker's meaning must be clear immediately. There should be little of the subtlety or multi-layered meanings we sometimes find in written works.

When most of us are asked to write a speech, however, our finished product ends up looking—and reading—more like an essay. That's understandable, because most of us have taken college courses in how to write essays, and almost none of us have taken courses in how to write speeches. Moreover, our experience in business and other institutions lies mainly in writing essaylike documents: letters, memoranda, and reports.

When you're preparing a presentation, there's nothing wrong with writing an essay first. In fact, I recommend it. But when the essay is finished, the job is not done. You then have to revise it, simplify it, and make it conversational. That is, you have to turn it into a speech, a form that lends itself to oral delivery.

BILLIONS? MILLIONS?

Presentations direct themselves primarily to the ear. Written documents are directed to our eyes, very sensitive organs.

But as I've indicated in Chapter 6, our ears don't always pick up information clearly. For example, if a speaker talks about "billions" of dollars, some of the audience might hear "millions," some "trillions," and some, distracted by other concerns or extraneous noises, might hear nothing at all.

PRESENTATIONS AND OTHER THINGS THAT GO BUMP IN THE NIGHT

In preparing remarks, it's essential to make sure they're heard and understood. Listening to an abstract, jargon-filled, data-laden speech can be disorienting. It can leave the listener feeling like a house guest looking for the bathroom and having to walk through darkened, furniture-filled rooms and hallways booby-trapped with sleeping animals and children's toys.

Audiences have great problems with essay-like presentations that suffer from pretentiousness. In other words, a bad essay makes an even worse presentation. Let's look at some examples of essays masquerading as speeches.

EXAMPLE #1: THE CHANCELLOR SAYS A MOUTHFUL

The first one is from a speech by a former chancellor of a major university. In a passage typical of his remarks, he says, "It seems to me that the growing gap between our technological culture and the level of general understanding of technology constitutes a kind of 'literacy crisis' whose effects will be increasingly apparent in the years ahead."

As an oral statement, what's wrong with the chancellor's words? Let me count the ways.

- The sentence has 36 words in it—too many for the speaker to say comfortably and for an audience to grasp.

- Many of the words used are unnecessary; for example, the first five words ("It seems to me that") add nothing; the phrase "kind of" is superfluous; and the last four words ("in the years ahead") are not necessary if the speaker just says the gap *will* grow.

- It's loaded with abstractions ("technological culture . . . literacy crisis") and polysyllables.

- It ends not with his key phrase "literacy crisis," but with the anticlimactic add-on ("whose effect will be increasingly apparent in the years ahead").

The chancellor's statement is a yawner, an example of *blunted* eloquence. Its diction and syntax convey not conviction, but pomposity. Even the initially interesting reference to a "literacy crisis" seems ultimately to be an attempt to inflate an essentially empty subject.

Could the Chancellor's Statement Have Been Saved?

What could the chancellor have done to turn his statement into plain, effective English? One way is to put his raw, meandering thoughts into simpler language.

The Editor's "Fix"

Besides rethinking his subject, the chancellor might have sought the help of a good editor. One editorial "fix" for the chancellor's statement would have been to take out the unnecessary words.

With this approach, his remarks would read as follows (with the words in brackets eliminated and the letters and words in parentheses inserted): [It seems to me that] The gap between our technological culture and (most Americans') understanding of technology [constitutes a kind of 'literacy crisis' whose effect will be increasingly apparent in the years ahead] will (grow wider).

When Less Is More

The revised statement contains 15 words. That's a 60 percent reduction over the 36 words in the chancellor's original statement. The new sentence is clearer and more understandable, reflecting once again the point that **in speech less usually is more.**

The Mental Fix

The main problem with the chancellor's original statement, however, is not a lack of editing. It's a lack of thinking about the subject and a lack of consideration for the audience. For example, what is this "technological culture" to which he refers? Does he mean computers and modern telecommunications? If so, he should say what he means.

What if he had said: In modern work and education, computers are vital. But as computers become more and more sophisticated, fewer Americans know how to use them.

Where the chancellor's statement had 36 words, this new one has 23. What if he protested that the new statement is not what he wanted to say (a protest this author would disbelieve)? An appropriate response would be that his original version didn't say much of anything.

EXAMPLE #2: ANOTHER ARGUMENT FOR SILENCE

Let's look briefly at another example of a speech that's really an essay, this one from the publication *Vital Speeches of the Day*: "There are three ways that the underlying stagnation of the world economy could produce a full-fledged crisis. In ascending order of severity, these are: (1) the threat of trade conflict akin to the interwar period, (2) the exchange rate problem and generalized international monetary instability and (3) the debt problem, with its attendant risks for the financial system at both the global and national levels. Each of these problems is extremely serious in its own right, but it is their cumulative impact and the inter-relationships among them that further intensify the perilous nature of the overall situation."

Quick, Reader, What Was Problem #2?

The "overall situation" (a nice redundancy) is no more perilous than the preceding author's future as a public speaker. He tells us the three problems he identifies are "extremely serious," but he presents them in such a turgid way that few people could remember any of them.

Listening to this kind of presentation is like walking through a corn field or a Chevrolet plant. Everything looks the same. Nothing leaps out at us. The presentation drones on with its rhetoric about interrelationships and "cumulative impacts," and the audience's eyes glaze over.

The two mini-essays I've quoted don't make good speeches. In fact, they don't make good essays. They use more than twice as many words as they should, and the words they use (mostly abstractions) have little effect on readers or listeners. Thus, *they lack the economy and the intensity characteristic of all good communications, oral or written.*

WHY GOOD PEOPLE WRITE SUCH BAD THINGS

What is it that happens to people which makes them produce material like those I've quoted? I believe it's a kind of mental paralysis that afflicts many people who, pen in hand, stare at a blank page.

Let me characterize this problem with an anecdote. Once upon a time I worked at a large financial services company. Someone asked me if I would read and comment on a memo that was to go to the chairman of the board. I read the piece, made a few minor suggestions, and said I thought it was ready to go.

The individual looked at me, shook his head, and said, "No. It's not ready to send yet. I still have to put in the big words."

His point was that a memo for the Big Boss could not go upstairs without Big Words.

The belief that Big Words and Long Sentences indicate intelligence has generated a lot of bad speeches. It's the cause behind presentations that use words like "parameters" (misused in cases where "perimeters" would be correct), "contraindications," and "impacted positively on earnings." People generally talk that way because they think it's expected. They think it makes their remarks sound more important than they are.

Those individuals who want to prepare good presentations, however, have to get that assumption out of their heads. They have to realize that good verbal communications rely almost exclusively on subject-verb-object constructions, on simple words and basic syntax.

The Example of Lee Iacocca

As an illustration of the kind of language that works in speeches, consider Lee Iacocca's remarks to the National Education Association. In his talk, he criticized America's grotesque surplus of lawyers compared to its shortage of engineers.

Iacocca told the educators: "How about if we'd just stop suing each other at the drop of a hat? Would that make us more competitive? Japan graduates *ten engineers* for every lawyer, and we graduate *ten lawyers* for every engineer. Does that tell you something? They train people to build a better mousetrap, and we train people to sue the guy with the mousetrap. So who's the smart guy?"

Look at Iacocca's first sentence. It contains 15 words, but 12 of them have one syllable! In fact, the only words in the entire passage that have more than two syllables are "competitive," "graduates" and "engineer(s)." Three of his sentences are punchy rhetorical questions—a technique he uses regularly. Iacocca's oratory is popular, perhaps because people have recognized it as the sound of an authentic human voice.

PENNSYLVANIA'S PREMIER PRESENTER

One elected official who knows the difference between an essay and a presentation is Pennsylvania state legislator Richard Snyder. Year-in and year-out Snyder gives some of the best presentations in America. He exemplifies the "less is more" approach to speaking.

In one speech, he spoke about the many people who don't like what they see and hear on television. His advice: "Buy earmuffs and postage stamps." The earmuffs are to tune out the messages people don't like. The postage stamps are to put onto their letters of complaint.

In this regard, Snyder says, "You probably expect me to advise you to write the networks. No. That would be wasted time. You don't pay the networks. Their sponsors do. So write the sponsors."

Note how Snyder boils down his message. One sentence consists of one word ("No."). Four other sentences are five words or less. This helps give his remarks a relentless intensity and clarity. We understand what he's saying because he's done so much work to make his message clear.

MARK TWAIN: THE LESS YOU WANT, THE MORE WORK IT TAKES

When someone asked him how long it would take to prepare a speech, Mark Twain put it this way: "It depends on how long the speech is to be. If you want a one-hour speech, it will take a couple of hours. But if you want a ten-minute speech, it will take about two days."

It takes time and effort to achieve the kind of focus and intensity I've called blunt eloquence. It's a paradox: The more conversational and simple a presentation is, the more time it took to prepare it.

THE INITIAL ESSAY: CLEAR AND COHERENT, BUT NOT YET A PRESENTATION

The initial essay written for a presentation should be clear and coherent. Editing it into a speech should make it more so. To exemplify this process, I've taken a short essay—actually, a "letter to the editor"—that appeared in *The New York Times* in August 1991. The letter dealt with President Bush's proposal to reduce the amount of U.S. land classified as "wetlands," areas covered by water for a certain portion of the year. The letter, written by David Henderson, follows.

> *To the Editor:*
> *"The Swamp President" (editorial, Aug. 14) is misleading. Of course, the Bush Administration's proposals to redefine wetlands will "result in wetland loss, at least by present standards." The capricious standards are themselves the problem. As much as half of the Eastern United States and perhaps 40 percent of drought-stricken California could be defined as wetlands under the current definition. The Administration's proposals are a timid first step toward injecting sanity into the policy.*
>
> *Contrary to your assertion, the Clean Water Act of 1972 protects not wetlands but "the navigable waters of the United States." The former Army Corps of Engineers wetland regulator, Bernard Goode, says the act was never intended to protect wetlands; regulators expanded their jurisdiction, including wetlands as a subset of "navigable waters."*

*Ideally, Mr. Goode says, regulators would define prop-
erty as wetlands only if the soil were saturated for at least
30 consecutive days a year; the new guidelines assume
that 21 days is long enough.*

*But this change is a good start. As the President says, "not
every puddle is a wetland."*

If You Didn't Agree with Henderson's Argument, You'll Especially Appreciate His Brevity

As a written piece, Henderson's letter is good. It's strong
and generally straightforward. It makes its point with brevity
and conviction. Like every good debater, Henderson takes a
controversial issue and tries for a quick argumentative
knock-out.

His letter does contain one cliché, "drought-stricken."
Maybe Henderson might have tried "drought-ridden." And
the last sentence in the first paragraph has a redundancy,
"defined . . . under the current definition." Perhaps he might
have said: ". . . would fit the current definition of wetlands."

If Henderson's letter were an oral presentation, it would
be less satisfactory. Let's look at his piece's shortcomings *if
it had been cast as a speech.*

Paragraph One

For an American audience (but not a British one), the
phrase "Of course" would sound overly formal. Moreover, the
speaker might trip on "capricious standards," which contains many "s" sounds. Also, the fact that one passage is
quoted would not be evident in an oral presentation. Finally,
"defined . . . under the current definition" would sound
clumsy when spoken. (In fact, reading aloud is a good way
to catch deficiencies in either the written or spoken word.)

Second Paragraph

No speaker this side of the British House of Lords says things like "contrary to your assertion"; we'd say "you're wrong about, etc." The quoted material in paragraph two would not be distinguishable from the words preceding and following it. The passive voice ("was never intended") hides its subject. Is he referring to Congress' intention? If so, it would strengthen the point to say so. The word "subset" is (1) hard to say; and (2) unfamiliar to most people, some of whom might hear it as "sunset."

Third Paragraph

The "Ideally, Mr. Goode says," segment is a written construction. In speech, it sounds stiff and formal. (Read it aloud, and you'll see what I mean.) The "were saturated" passive construction tends to drain strength from the passage. Also, the key words in the last sentence may be 21 days, not the somewhat anti-climactic "long enough."

Fourth Paragraph

The "not every puddle is a wetland" line is a good one. Frankly, it's the kind of simplification (wetlands' proponents would say "gross oversimplification") that works well in oral presentations. However, try saying it this way, "As the President says, we shouldn't confuse wetlands . . . with puddles." This ends the statement on the "punch word," *puddles.*

From Essay . . . To Speech

With the changes I've suggested, the Henderson letter might look this way as a speech text (given below in italics), perhaps one read to the *Times'* editorial board:

Your editorial on "The Swamp President" misses the point. Yes, the Bush Administration's proposals to redefine wetlands will—in your editorial's words—"result in wetland loss, at least by present federal standards." But it's just those arbitrary standards that are the problem.

Under current standards, guess how much of the eastern United States would qualify as wetlands. About 50 percent! And in drought-ridden California it's roughly 40 percent. The Administration is only trying to bring some sanity to wetlands definitions.

Your editorial says The Clean Water Act protects wetlands. You're just plain wrong. It protects—in the words of the Act—"the navigable waters of the United States." (Pause)

Listen to what Bernard Goode says—the man who used to regulate wetlands for the Army Corps of Engineers. He says Congress never intended the Clean Water Act to protect wetlands. Goode says the group that brought wetlands under that Act's provisions was the regulators.

Mr. Goode defines a wetland as having soil saturation for 30 consecutive days a year. The Bush Administration's guidelines are 21 days a year. That's a start.

As the President says, we shouldn't confuse wetlands . . . with puddles. (An alternative ending: As the President says, we shouldn't confuse wetlands . . . with mudholes.)

A speech has a kind of relentlessness that we generally don't find in essays. It tries not for suggestiveness and multiple meanings but for instant understanding.

WHAT IF YOU WANT TO USE NOTE CARDS RATHER THAN A FULL SPEECH TEXT?

What if you wanted to do the presentation by using note cards? Before you do your essay, you will want to make some rough notes. Then, write the presentation out as an essay.

The next step is to turn it into a speech. Finally, do your note cards. In a sense, you will have come "full circle."

The importance of the presentation will determine how rigorously you follow this procedure. Doing the essay is essential. It will give you an overall look at the topic and how you propose to develop it. Turning the essay into a speech will bring you closer to the actual presentation. It will allow you to hear and, if you videotape your practice session(s), to see how your performance goes.

THE PEOPLE/PAPER RATIO

As a general rule, the more people you have in your audience, the more "paper" that's permissible. For a one-on-one with the boss, you might not use any notes (although you may have used them in your preparation). To make some brief comments at a business meeting, you'd probably use a few note cards. For a formal presentation (say, a luncheon speech) at a business or civic organization, you might use a prepared speech.

Some people treat the "cards or speech" question as if it were an eternal dilemma. The question is moot. It doesn't matter greatly whether you rely on notes or a speech script.

That is, if you accept this book's advocacy of thorough preparation, you will be successful using either notes or a speech text. Before you make your presentation, you should know exactly what you want to say, and you should have a good idea how your audience will respond. Moreover, you should have revised, and rehearsed, your presentation so that you're completely comfortable with it. You should know exactly what you want to say and be ready to answer any questions the audience might ask.

Conventional Wisdom Strikes Out Again

Some speech coaches swear by note cards. They believe cards make for a more conversational, natural, spontaneous presentation. As readers of this book suspect, I think such coaches are wrong. Ronald Reagan almost always used speech texts. Yet his presentations were as down-home and conversational as a back-porch chat. They used language that came naturally to Reagan. They reflected the way he thought and felt. Note cards would not have made President Reagan seem any more conversational.

Written Speeches: Make Them
Sound Spontaneous, Natural

By the same token, a written speech should not sound flat and formal. It should be written in conversational language. It should reflect the speaker's views and personality. And the speaker's intonations and emphases should reinforce the oral content of the presentation.

Done well, note-card presentations will not differ much from "full-text" presentations. They both will reflect the careful preparation that's going into them. In fact, I've heard speakers praised for their "off-the-cuff" speeches when, without the audience detecting it, they've used a speech text.

NOTE CARDS: PLUSES AND MINUSES

Some people prefer note cards because they're less obtrusive. They fit easily into a pocket or the palm of your hand. If you're concerned about preserving the illusion of spontaneity, the audience is less apt to notice cards than they are a relatively bulky speech.

Putting It on Paper: Harold Puts
the Hammer Down

Whether you use speech texts or note cards, it's important to get presentations down on paper. The speaker can then tinker with the text, move passages around, change the organization, and try out alternative words and phrasing. If presentations exist only "in our head," it takes mental gymnastics to make the changes and adjustments necessary to perfect them.

One corporate official who did this effectively was Harold Hammer, an executive vice president at Gulf Oil. When Hammer had to make a speech, he'd discuss it with Gulf speech writer Bob Steck, who would then prepare a draft. Steck knew his client's likes and dislikes very well, and he'd invariably put together a good speech and send it to Hammer.

Then Hammer would call Steck and me (Steck's boss) up to his office. The Gulf executive would read the speech aloud. He'd stop frequently after a passage and ask questions—as much of himself as of us. Questions would include: "Do I really agree with that point? But how would I put it? What words would I use?" He would compose on the spot, making changes as he went along.

Hammer had an (undeserved) reputation as something of Gulf's corporate ogre. He was a very formal man, an image somewhat undercut in our sessions as speech pages became strewn about. He was also extremely intelligent and not one to suffer fools gladly. Steck and I would manifest our most un-foollike demeanors.

What was Hammer doing as he sharp-penciled his way through Steck's draft? He was making the speech his own. He was also simplifying the language, making it truer to his preferred mode of expression.

Hammer was also using the two of us for an early rehearsal. He frequently asked us how a certain passage sounded. Sometimes he'd try two or more ways of expressing an idea and ask us which we preferred.

Sometimes these sessions would last for more than an hour, an eternity for an executive to spend with speech writers. But Hammer regarded this time as well spent. He realized that the speech text we gave him was just a starting point. The draft was material for him to mold into the form he wanted.

When he was finished going over the speech, he had considered every word in it. At that point, it didn't matter greatly whether he used a speech text or note cards. In either case, he would have had full control over his material.

WHAT ABOUT MEMORIZING PRESENTATIONS?

Most speech experts advise against memorizing presentations. When speakers memorize their remarks, they tend to present them with all the animation of small girls and boys reciting "The Gettysburg Address" at school assemblies. That's because memorization causes most people to focus on verbal accuracy rather than on verbal effectiveness.

Memorization also contains the potential for disaster. What if the presenter forgets a thought or two? In that case, the ensuing silence tends to "reverberate" through the hall.

Don't Memorize . . . Unless You're John Loewenberg

The only exception to the admonition against memorizing remarks is if you do it extremely well. John Loewenberg, a senior vice president at Aetna, gave slide presentations. He memorized not only his remarks, but also which slides went with which remarks. That meant he never had to look at his slides—or at a text.

The one problem I saw with Loewenberg's approach was that the audience sometimes found his skill distracting. Instead of listening to what he said, they sat there wondering how he did it.

Most people won't want to memorize their remarks. Whether they use a speech text or note cards, however, *they should know their presentation extremely well.* The best way to do that is through rigorous editing of what they want to say and through regular practice, or rehearsal.

GOOD PRESENTATIONS ARE MADE, NOT BORN

Make it brief. Make it simple. Make it clear. In doing these three things, your presentation will reflect the work you've put into it. It will show that you've thought about your subject, that you've achieved a clear understanding of it, and that you've put it into terms you can handle—and your audience can understand.

Points to Remember:

- Write an essay as the basis for your speech text or note cards.
- Direct your presentation to the audience's ears by using words and ideas that are easily understandable.
- Prepare your presentation thoroughly; it won't matter if you use a full speech text or note cards.
- Avoid delivering memorized material (unless you do it exceptionally well).
- Be brief, simple, and clear in every presentation you prepare.

14

FEAR:
NAMING THE NAMELESS,
REASONING WITH
THE UNREASONING

"The only thing we have to fear is fear itself . . . nameless, unreasoning fear." (Franklin D. Roosevelt, First Inaugural Address)

Many books on presentations start with a chapter on fear. By doing so, they give fear of public speaking special prominence. They also imply that fear (and its emotional cousin, "anxiety") exist in and of themselves, apart from other aspects of presentations.

We tend to fear the unknown. By taking the mystery—and much of the emotion—out of presentations, we drive out fear.

WHAT SPEAKERS ARE AFRAID OF

When people are asked to identify the reasons for their fear of making presentations, they focus either on content or on delivery. On the one hand, they say they fear that the audience won't like or understand what they say. Perhaps, they suggest, the audience might even walk out on them.

Or, on the other hand, they say they fear forgetting the material or delivering it poorly.

(Charlie Kittrell, former executive vice president of Phillips Petroleum, once delivered a presentation making the case for higher energy prices. His remarks angered a woman in the audience who stood up and stomped out of the hall. Along with the audience, Kittrell watched her departure. Then, adopting the down-home tones of his native Arkansas, Kittrell said, "My daddy said never to pay any mind when people walked out on you. He told me, 'Charlie, the only time to worry is when the audience starts walking *toward* you.'" The audience howled.)

SOME BASIC POINTS ABOUT PRESENTATIONS AND FEAR

All speakers want to deliver good presentations. Generally, they fail to do so because they don't know either what to talk about or how to deliver their message effectively. They don't know the steps they can take to minimize the chance of failure and thus eliminate the presence of fear.

Talk Your Way to the Top outlines exactly those steps. This is a book about proceeding systematically to ensure that you make effective presentations.

But what if you don't? What if the audience doesn't heed your call to action? What if it falls asleep? In other words, what if you fire your best shots and they start imploding?

Don't Touch That Red Button!

Remember, making a presentation is not the same as deciding whether to launch a nuclear war, or to commute a death sentence. It's an effort to communicate, to share your views and feelings with an audience. Sometimes, to paraphrase poet Robert Burns, the best-intentioned presentations "gang aft agley" (go astray).

If you fail, don't contemplate suicide. Don't start planning to move to a faraway community. Instead, lick your wounds and then make a dispassionate examination of why the communication didn't succeed.

For example, did you misjudge your audience's values and beliefs? In your call to action, were you asking them to do more than you could have reasonably expected them to do? Were the points you used to support your call to action not compelling enough? Ultimately, were you delivering a message you yourself didn't believe in wholeheartedly?

An Approach That's Not Recommended

Excessive fear of speaking in public can drive people to distraction, and even to drink. Consider the hero of Kingsley Amis' book *Lucky Jim*. He's asked to give a speech at an all-college meeting on his "special subject," The Economic Influences of the Developments in Shipbuilding Techniques, 1450 to 1485.

Jim has a few problems with this assignment, which he can't turn down because of his tenuous (and untenured) role at a second-rate British college. He doesn't like his department head or his colleagues. He doesn't much like teaching, although it's apparently all he can do. He especially doesn't like his special subject, which he finds as boring as it sounds. Least of all does he like speaking in public, which frightens him.

Before his appearance, Jim fortifies himself with ample doses of "octuple" whiskies. He also asks a friend to help him out with some strategem if the presentation goes as badly as he thinks it might.

The presentation goes horribly. Jim is dead drunk. His mouth is dry, his throat constricted, his diction reminiscent of speaking in tongues. The faces in the audience swim before him, especially the disapproving visage of his department head.

He speeds up the pace of his presentation, hoping to get through it. Almost against his will, he begins mimicking his department head's distinctive voice. Then he starts delivering his text as if it were a Hitlerian harangue. Suddenly, lightheaded and faint, Jim stops speaking. Meanwhile, members of the audience have become very alarmed by his behavior.

His associate in the audience sees that Jim is in trouble. So the friend groans, clutches his chest, and pitches forward, feigning a faint. Simultaneously, Jim collapses and falls on his face.

Even if you have a willing co-conspirator and an unlimited supply of spirits, Jim's approach is not recommended.

ANOTHER APPROACH TO HANDLING A STRESSFUL SITUATION

In contrast to Jim's handling of his moment of truth, let's look at the behavior of another young man, an individual facing a much more stressful situation than the one encountered by "Lucky" Jim. This was a young Air Force captain who was profiled on television during the Gulf War. His mission was to bomb Baghdad on the first night of the war.

What awaited him? The most intense anti-aircraft fire in the history of aerial combat. The untender mercies of the Iraqis if he were to be shot down and taken captive. The perils of possible injury or death.

How did he respond? He walked out to the tarmac and waited for mechanics to ready his plane. As he watched them complete their duties, he showed no discernible emotions. The only sign of concern was an indirect one: He licked his lips once. And then he got into the plane, taxied down the runway, and headed north to bomb the Iraqi capital.

Should Jim Have Delivered His Remarks from a Cockpit?

Of course, speaking in public and flying a jet plane in combat are not comparable. At worst, Jim faces public embarrassment and unemployment. The fighter pilot faces much more serious threats. Jim's task is that most natural of human activities, talking to people. The pilot's job is highly unnatural: flying a heavier-than-air craft into a sky filled with anti-aircraft fire and computer-guided missiles.

So why, we ask, is Jim petrified, while the Air Force captain is the picture of emotional control? The answer lies in professionalism. In undertaking his task, Jim did not approach it as a professional; the fighter pilot did.

Where Jim Went Wrong

Jim went wrong in not focusing on his task: making an effective presentation; instead, he focused on himself, which is the recipe for generating fear and self-doubt. As we learn in Amis' book, Jim did not see his "special subject" as interesting. He did not see that Medieval Ship Building had any relevance to him, let alone to anyone else. He had chosen his academic specialty by default.

In his remarks, he didn't have any call to action, and he didn't really consider his topic in light of the audience's beliefs and attitudes. He didn't ask the audience to reconsider medieval shipbuilding or to view its late fifteenth-century version in a new historical light. He didn't ask them to see its effect on the building of the New World.

In addition, he didn't attempt to achieve even an academic equivalent of "blunt eloquence." He didn't try to give his presentation verbal energy and economy. Needless to say, he spent so much time worrying about the presentation that he didn't have an opportunity to practice and polish it.

The result: He read the audience an essay. Instead of giving a tired topic a shot of adrenaline, he fed the audience a verbal soporific.

Depressed by the subject and the circumstances of his talk, Jim gulped down liberal quantities of alcohol, a depressant. In that way, he made sure that his mental distress was accompanied by physical deterioration.

Little wonder that Jim's presentation turned out to be a disaster, confirming his worst fears.

THE CAPTAIN OFFERS A CONTRAST

Contrast Jim's lack of preparation with that of our real-life Air Force captain. Because of the officer's youth, we can assume he had never been in combat before. What's striking about him and the breed of individuals he represents is their task orientation.

They are focused on accomplishing their mission, on heeding their own call to action. They are the product of especially rigorous training, of endless takeoffs, combat maneuvers, and landings. Through what they call "training" (and the presenter calls "rehearsal"), they practice their craft.

Who can doubt that the Air Force captain did his own form of "audience analysis"? That he studied the enemy's defensive capabilities. That he knew his targets as if they were imprinted on his brain.

Unlike Jim, the captain was the essence of professionalism, of knowledge and skill applied with style.

The more we concentrate on a task, the more professionally we approach it, the less time we have to focus on our fears. In her fine book *St. Maybe*, author Anne Tyler describes the concentration of highly skilled furniture makers. She sees them as typical of individuals dedicating themselves to an "all-consuming task that left no room for extraneous thoughts."

IT MAY SURPRISE YOU, BUT . . . "FEAR OF SPEAKING" IS OVERRATED

That kind of total absorption is what this book advocates. In showing how to proceed systematically in making good presentations, this book seeks to build presenters' confidence. That confidence is the element which dissolves fear.

SOME TECHNIQUES FOR OVERCOMING PRESENTATION FEAR

There are a number of techniques people use to ward off the fear of making presentations. Any good book on stress management will give you a number of suggestions for warding off fear and stress. For example, rotating your neck muscles before you go on the podium will help loosen tight muscles in the head area. Shrugging your shoulders will have a similar effect. In addition, some people find that yawning a few times helps to loosen constricted vocal cords. These kinds of symptomatic relief allow us to manage stress.

Don't Settle For Managing Stress—Avoid It

However, this book downplays *managing* stress and emphasizes *avoiding* stress. Have a provocative message and a strong call to action; analyze what your audience knows and believes about your topic; prepare a persuasive presentation; practice (rehearse) it faithfully.

Do Those Things and Watch Fear Truly Strike Out

If you do those things, you will automatically decrease any fear or stress you might have. You will be like my Gulf War Air Force captain. You will have done everything you can do to accomplish your mission. No one will ask any more of you, and you should ask no more of yourself. Give it your all, and you've given it everything it deserves.

A PRESENTATION AS A WORK OF ARTIFICE

We need to think of a presentation as a product, as a task we complete. It's produced by artifice, and the result is an artifact that we can examine (through taping) and continue to modify and improve through a systematic effort.

For many reasons, it's important to concentrate less on delivery than on content. One reason is that most speakers' fears relate to questions of delivery. They worry that the audience is going to focus on the speaker rather than on the message. Thus, people worry about how listeners will react to their accents, their diction, their clothing, and so on.

Build a good message, and the audience will come around.

Remember: the Audience Looks in the Same Mirror You Do

Think about it: Was Franklin Roosevelt fearful about speaking in public? The historians confirm our impression that the answer was no. Why not? One reason was that, unlike his predecessors Coolidge and Hoover, he sought out opportunities to speak.

Second, Roosevelt believed in the message he delivered. That is evident in the energy and conviction his remarks demonstrated.

A third factor was that, even though Roosevelt relied on professional speech writers, he reportedly devoted a good deal of effort and energy to his speeches. He revised important speech drafts, seeking to make them more conversational and to heighten their effect on his audience.

A *LITTLE* ANXIETY CAN BE A PLUS

Having some anxiety about speaking in public is natural. In fact, it can be a positive force, impelling us to make the effort to give effective presentations. As Aetna CEO Ron Compton once put it, "I'm a little scared, but that's good, because it keeps me on edge, makes me alert, and helps me perform up to my best."

Asked about fear of speaking in public, evangelist Billy Graham admitted, "I still get nervous when I speak. A small audience is worse than a large crowd." Graham has made more than 10,000 presentations. Perhaps the passion with which he invests his presentations results, in part, from his efforts to overcome fear.

If you follow the principles set out in this book, you will have the kind of total focus we find in the consummate craftsperson. In that case, you will turn anxiety into intensity. You will transmute nervousness into conviction.

Overall, you will have given fear a name: lack of preparation. You will have reasoned away the unreasoning fear of failure through a commitment to the factors that produce success. Call it positive thinking if you wish, but it's really *positive action.*

Points to Remember:

- Drive out fear by taking the mystery out of your presentations.

- Accomplish that end by knowing your subject and your audience inside-out, practicing your presentation assiduously, and believing firmly in your message.

- Concentrate on your task—delivering a powerful message—so fully that you will have no time or emotional energy to expend on excessive fear.

- Channel whatever fear remains into intensity.

15

EFFECTIVE COMMUNICATION: THE ART OF REMAKING YOURSELF

Improving your ability to communicate means gaining control over a vital aspect of your life.

A PROFESSOR WHO PRACTICED WHAT HE PROFESSED

Rhodes Scholar, author, and University of Georgia Distinguished Professor Calvin Brown was a stickler for excellence. He also had little tolerance for student self-indulgence. When a student questioned his grade on a comparative literature paper, Brown justified it by saying the paper manifested poor scholarship.

"But, Dr. Brown," the student said, "I don't want to be a scholar. *I just want to be myself.*"

Brown gave the student a critical look and said, "Surely you can aim higher than *that.*"

"AIM HIGH" AND YOU CAN SCALE ANY HEIGHTS

Talk Your Way to the Top is not a book that advocates just being yourself. It recommends ways you can *improve* yourself in the important area of making presentations. It provides a systematic approach to strengthening a capacity you already have: the ability to communicate.

Q[UALITY] = T[IME] X YOU

This book takes the view that the quality of your presentations depends on the time you put into them: $Q = T \times Y$. Don't spend a lot of time worrying about how your presentations will be received. Spend the time making sure that you don't have anything to worry about. That is, spend the time making sure the presentations are good.

BUT IF HE'S SUCH A BAD PRESENTER, WHY IS HE SO RICH?

Of course some people who make terrible presentations don't seem to have suffered from that fact, socially or financially. For example, I attended a presentation given by a noted doctor/entrepreneur. This gentleman had graduated from two major universities. He had launched a health-care business that seemed well on its way to making him a megamillionaire. He gave one of the worst presentations I've ever heard.

One of Those Speeches Where You Wonder: Is There Any Way I Could Crawl Out of the Hall Without Being Seen?

In his remarks, he used medical jargon that mystified half the audience. Part of the time he spoke with his back to his listeners, making it nearly impossible to hear what he was saying. When the attendees could hear him, the speaker made generalizations that seemed highly dubious (for example, "More than half of all medical care given today is unnecessary"). At other times, he spoke down to the audience, implying how lucky we were to have a great man like him addressing us. For his visual aids, he used Vu-graphs that were so loaded with text they were unreadable. His charts and graphs were not eye-catching. Some of his visuals were in three shades of green, giving them almost no visual distinction. On two occasions, he indicated that he hadn't seen some of the Vu-graphs he was using. When he put them up on the screen, he gawked at them.

Was That the Speaker's Call for Action, Or Was It the Audience Calling for Help?

The speaker's remarks had no call to action. There was no sign he had considered the needs and views of his audience. There was no evidence he had rehearsed the remarks. The presentation began and ended in disarray, and from their remarks later, members of the audience resented the speaker's taking their time.

The presentation aside, from all appearances the speaker was a business success. But one wonders if appearances could be deceiving. Would a speaker who pays so little attention to a major presentation give more heed to his business? Perhaps. But in a business (health-care) that depends on selling patients and health-care professionals on its benefits, the doctor was a poor salesman.

HOW CAN YOU AVOID EMULATING THE DOCTOR'S POOR PERFORMANCE?

People become good communicators in much the same way that people become good bowlers, or good parents, or good writers. They learn the fundamentals of good performance. They practice their task faithfully. They learn from their mistakes. They persuade themselves (visualization) that they can do their task well, and they go and do it.

RICHARD GODOWNE AND THE QUALITIES
OF A SUPERB PRESENTATION

Contrast the doctor's poor performance with the approach exemplified by Richard Godowne, head of the Industrial Biotechnology Association. In a presentation he gave, Godowne made a powerful case for supporting biotechnology and genetic research.

His presentation was smooth and professional. He'd obviously rehearsed it well, as illustrated by his easy use of difficult words like "panegryric" and "opthalmic." He used the example of human growth hormone (given to children who would otherwise remain severely undersized) to illustrate the importance of genetic engineering.

After he heard Godowne's presentation, a friend of mine who's an outstanding speech writer and speech teacher said: "I wish I had a tape of his remarks. I'd use it in my public-speaking classes."

THE CEOS: GOOD COMMUNICATIONS
ARE PART OF THEIR JOB DESCRIPTIONS

As I've suggested, the CEOs are not necessarily better communicators than you and I. But most of them have an unerring ability to "go to the heart of the matter." They zero in on subjects, capturing their essence.

BILL GATES: THE BILLIONAIRE AS COMMUNICATOR

We see this no-nonsense style in Bill Gates, CEO of Microsoft, and the most powerful individual in the computer software business. In an interview, Gates talked about the "aesthetic" of computer programming and the value some engineers will place on programs they create. He then added, "But there is in the end a test of 'Does it work, is it fast, is it small, does it get it [the job] done?' "

Gates's criteria for engineers also apply to presenters. He is speaking about simplicity, economy, and effectivenss.

These are admirable goals for any presentation, as they are for any engineering project.

The best CEOs take this approach to their presentations. In fact, their effort to achieve a clear understanding of issues is what set them apart from their competitors. Their leadership rests largely on their understanding of what they're talking about.

CEOS ARE A LOT OF THINGS . . . AND NOW IT TURNS OUT THEY'RE ALSO METAPHORS

In this book, I've used business executives—the CEOs—as examples of strong communicators. Not all successful executives are good communicators, but most are. It's part of their job description.

WE LEAD NOT ONLY WITH DEEDS, BUT WITH WORDS

The CEOs are a metaphor for leaders in any organization. Leadership is largely a matter of outlining issues, identifying options, and laying out strategies. All these qualities depend on communication, on words. The man or woman who is "good with words" has an edge in life.

This book tells how to gain that edge. The principles it has outlined are ones you can—and should—begin using immediately. Techniques like the call to action, blunt eloquence, audience analysis, and controlling a dialogue are ones you can use every day. You should find them helpful every time you communicate, whether it's with your doctor, your spouse, your business trade association, or your political party's national convention.

Talk Your Way to the Top is about taking control of your presentations—and every conversational situation is a presentation of a sort. As you seize control of your language, you tend to become a dominant force in social and economic situations. People begin to look to you for guidance and leadership.

At that point, you're well on your way in talking yourself to the top. You may not become a CEO of a major corporation. But you will have learned one major secret to their progress: the effective use of words is the foundation of success.

Points to Remember:

- Improve your ability to communicate, and you gain greater control over your life.

- Three things are vital to such improvement: practice . . . practice . . . and more practice.

- Show your emerging leadership ability through your capacity to outline issues, identify options, and articulate strategies.

INDEX